"*Hayfield's* Bisexual and Pansexual Identities: Exploring and Challenging Invisibility and Invalidation *is a much needed text both in studying plurisexualities and sexualities more broadly. Hayfield's text has a brilliant clarity and breadth, giving much needed academic attention to bisexual identities, and also sexual identities not commonly studied including asexuality and pansexuality. Its particular strengths lie in characterising the complex and disparate debates to impress upon the reader the invisibility and marginalisation of plurisexual identities. These points are accentuated through Hayfield's compelling usage of contemporary illustrations of plurisexual invisibility across media and society. This is an excellent and accessible resource for anyone with an interest in sexuality, across all levels of expertise.*"

Mx. Rosie Nelson, University of Bristol, U.K.

"*Nikki Hayfield's work on bi/pan/asexual invisibility is an essential resource on the documentation of the historical development and reinforcement of this invisibility and its modern manifestations and consequences. This text weaves together decades of research into a useful and impactful narrative that can support the future visibility of these communities.*"

Corey Flanders, Dept of Psychology and Education,
Mount Holyoke College, U.S.

BISEXUAL AND PANSEXUAL IDENTITIES

This book explores the invisibility and invalidation of bisexuality from the past to the present, and is unique in extending the discussion to focus on contemporary and emerging identities. Nikki Hayfield draws on research from psychology and the social sciences to offer a detailed and in-depth exploration of the invisibility and invalidation of bisexuality, pansexuality, and asexuality.

The book discusses how early sexologists understood gender and sexuality within a binary model and how this provided the underpinnings of bisexual invisibility. The existing research on biphobia and bisexual marginalisation is synthesised to explore how bisexuality has often come to be invisible or invalidated. Hayfield then evidences clear examples of the invisibility and invalidation of bisexuality, pansexuality, and asexuality within education, employment, mainstream mass media, and the wider culture. Throughout the book there is consideration of the impact that this invisibility and invalidation has on people's sense of identity and on their health and well-being. It concludes with a discussion of how bisexuality, pansexuality, and asexuality have become somewhat more visible than in the past and the potential that visibility holds for recognition and representation.

This is fascinating reading for students and academics interested in bisexuality, pansexuality, and asexual spectrum identities, and for those who have a personal interest in bisexuality, pansexuality, and asexuality.

Nikki Hayfield is a social psychologist whose research interests are in bisexualities, pansexualities, asexualities, and sexualities more widely. She has published research on a range of topics, including bisexual identities, marginalisation, and relationships.

GENDER AND SEXUALITIES IN PSYCHOLOGY
Series Editors: Elizabeth Peel and Elizabeth Stokoe

Gender and Sexualities in Psychology is a book series showcasing scholarly work over a wide range of areas within gender and sexualities in psychology, and the intersection of gender, feminism, sexualities, and LGBTQI psychology with other areas of the discipline.

The series includes theoretically and empirically informed scholarship, including critical, feminist, queer, trans, social, and intersectional perspectives, and encourages creative and innovative methodological approaches. The series adopts an inclusive approach to the discipline of psychology, as well as its cross-cutting relationship to related disciplines, and recognises diversity in research on genders and sexualities.

Titles in the series:

Bisexual and Pansexual Identities
Exploring and Challenging Invisibility and Invalidation, 1st Edition
Nikki Hayfield

Queer Ink
A Blotted History Towards Liberation
Katherine Hubbard

Reproductive Losses
Challenges to LGBTQ Family-Making
Christa Craven

Emergent Identities
New Sexualities, Genders and Relationships in a Digital Era
Rob Cover

For further information about this series please visit: www.routledge.com/Gender-and-Sexualities-in-Psychology/book-series/GSP

BISEXUAL AND PANSEXUAL IDENTITIES

Exploring and Challenging Invisibility and Invalidation

Nikki Hayfield

Routledge
Taylor & Francis Group

LONDON AND NEW YORK

First published 2021
by Routledge
2 Park Square, Milton Park, Abingdon, Oxon OX14 4RN

and by Routledge
52 Vanderbilt Avenue, New York, NY 10017

Routledge is an imprint of the Taylor & Francis Group, an informa business

British Library Cataloguing-in-Publication Data
A catalogue record for this book is available from the British Library

Library of Congress Cataloging-in-Publication Data
A catalog record has been requested for this book

ISBN: 978-1-138-61375-1 (hbk)
ISBN: 978-1-138-61377-5 (pbk)
ISBN: 978-0-429-46436-2 (ebk)

Typeset in Bembo
by Swales & Willis, Exeter, Devon, UK

CONTENTS

ACKNOWLEDGEMENTS

First, thanks to all those bisexual, pansexual, asexual, and plurisexual participants who have taken part in research and all the activists and academics who have helped make bisexuality, pansexuality, asexuality, and many other sexualities become (somewhat) more visible and validated than they once were.

I am very fortunate to have met – and done research with – the most amazing people. It's difficult to know where to start in acknowledging who they are and the contributions they have made to my thinking, understanding, and research interests.

First, I am incredibly grateful to the students I have taught and supervised. To work with young people is an honour and you constantly inspire me. I toed and froed and ummed and ahhed about whether or not to list specific names for fear of leaving others out, but there are some I have to mention. Karolína Křížová was perhaps the most dedicated student I have encountered and I am delighted that it all panned out well. Thom Winter-Gray provided lots of food for thought and I much enjoyed our meetings about feta cheese. And Alexander Sinclair, Caoimhe Green, Chloe Martin, Debbie Lovell, Emma Hoggett, Hana Nour-Elmi, Jade Southron, Kelly Fey, Kiri Wicks, Mollie Cross, and Sharon Shalini are just a few who I have supervised and with whom it was a particular joy to work in one way or another.

I was fortunate enough to be a student at the university where Victoria Clarke was teaching a module in *Critical Sexualities*. I quickly realised that sex and sexualities were a fascinating topic area – and one I hadn't considered it was possible to study until taking the module. I was taught and supervised by Victoria as both an undergraduate and postgraduate student. The influence that she has had on my thinking, my academic endeavours, and my career is phenomenal. She deserves lots of (biodegradable) glitter, (gluten-free) cake, and (pink fluffy) unicorns. Through her I also learnt an incredible amount about qualitative research methods and met Ginny Braun, who is always a delight. The Ant and Dec/French and Saunders/Mel and Sue of the qualitative psychology world are fantastic. If I hadn't known them, I wouldn't have had the opportunity to work with Gareth Terry, who is totally awesome, in the literal sense of the word. Some of the other lovely academics who I have particularly loved meeting and/or working with include Adam Jowett, Annukka Lahti, Bethan Jones, Caroline Huxley, Chris Campbell, Christian Klesse, Debra Gray, Emiel Maliepaard, Emma Dures, Emma Halliwell, Helen Bowes-Catton, Helen Malson, Irmgard Tischner, Matt Wood, Miltos Hadjiosif, Naomi Moller, Renate Baumgartner, Rosie Nelson, and Zoe Thomas. Thank you to you all, and to everyone at the University of the West of England, especially Chris Pawson, Jane Humphreys, Jennie Ferrell, Julie Kent, Kieran McCartan, and Peter Clegg. My thanks also go to Merl Storr.

A few personal mentions. To my parents, for being ever supportive. To Dan for listening a lot and making me laugh even more, and to Arthur for being the most fun ever, and to Louise and Graham and Alexia. I am of course concerned that I have left people out …

Thanks also to those who made this book possible – Liz Peel and Elizabeth Stokoe as series editors, Kirsten McLean (your research inspired me during my PhD such a lot) and an anonymous reviewer, and Eleanor Reedy and Alex Howard at Routledge.

1

INTRODUCTION

> Bisexuals cannot begin work on developing a political presence as long as people continue to equate their ontological status with that of unicorns.
>
> *(Capulet, 2010, p. 295)*

> I think at the moment it really is almost invisible. That it is this kind of unicorn identity that nobody takes seriously.
>
> *(Eddy, bisexual research participant)*

These quotes equate the visibility and validity of bisexuality with the idea of the mythical unicorn and capture a sense of how bisexual identities have often been invisible or invalidated. These are the themes which form the focus of this book. Bisexual activists and academics have commonly discussed the invisibility of bisexuality. They have written of how bisexuality has been omitted, silenced, dismissed, and erased within academia, lesbian and gay communities, and the wider society – both historically and contemporarily. Since the 1990s, authors have published books which have focused on acknowledging and addressing this invisibility, such as *Bisexuality: The Psychology and Politics of an Invisible Minority* (Firestein, 1996); *Becoming Visible: Counseling Bisexuals Across the Lifespan* (Firestein, 2007); and *Bisexuality: Theories, Research, and Recommendations for the Invisible Sexuality* (Swan & Habibi, 2018). The notion of bisexual invisibility has often been referred to but has not always been fully explored. This book is novel in offering a contemporary in-depth exploration of the invisibility of bisexuality, using specific examples of how and where in/visibility plays out, and the ways in which in/visibility and in/validity impact on bisexual people's experiences of their identities. This book is primarily about bisexuality, but is unique in extending the discussion to include recently emerging identities which also relate to attraction to more than one gender – including pansexuality, asexual spectrum identities such as panromantic and biromantic, and other plurisexualities.

To write a book about these identities and their invisibility and invalidation requires evidence. However, the present picture is one of relatively little research. This means that evidence is sometimes minimal and somewhat limited. Research and publications specifically on these identities have gradually been increasing – since the 1970s (see below) in relation to bisexuality, since the 1990s/2000s in relation to pansexual and other plurisexual identities, and since the early 2000s in relation to asexuality. However, asexual spectrum identities and other plurisexualities remain largely invisible within the academic literature (Gray & Moore, 2018). The available academic sources drawn on in the writing of this book inform its primary focus on bisexuality but I include other identities relating to attraction to more than one gender wherever possible to meaningfully do so. In the first part of this introductory chapter, I discuss changing understandings of sexualities and introduce readers to bisexuality, pansexuality and other plurisexualities, and asexuality/asexual spectrum identities. In the second part, I discuss invisibility and provide an overview of the contents of each chapter of this book.

Changing understandings of sexualities

Within Western societies, conceptualisations of sexualities have evolved, particularly over the last century. Early understandings of sexuality were based on a unipolar perspective, where only heterosexuality was understood to be valid or viable. As sexologists began to theorise sexuality, there was a shift to bipolar understandings where "heterosexuality" and "homosexuality" were recognised as two distinct identities. During the 1940s and 1950s, Kinsey's surveys demonstrated the variability and diversity of human sexual behaviour. Critically, Kinsey challenged the binary understandings of heterosexuality and homosexuality which had dominated within psychology and the wider society (Box 1.1) (Kinsey, Pomeroy, & Martin, 1948; Kinsey, Pomeroy, Martin, & Gebhard, 1953). These key researchers' ideas are explored in more depth in Chapter 2.

BOX 1.1 KEY TERMS: BINARY UNDERSTANDINGS

Binary understandings of sexuality arise from binary understandings of sex and gender. When sex and gender are understood as dichotomous – within what has been termed the heterosexual matrix – sexuality also becomes conceptualised as dichotomous (Butler, 1990/2006). In this either/or model heterosexuality and homosexuality are understood as mutually exclusive and as the only meaningful identity positions. Therefore, binary understandings validate heterosexuality and homosexuality but invalidate and erase bisexuality. Binary understandings have dominated within Western cultures and have underpinned much of the invisibility, marginalisation, and erasure of bisexuality as a viable or valid identity (e.g., Bowes-Catton, 2007; Firestein, 2007; McLean, 2008, 2018; Storr, 1999; see also Chapter 3). This may extend to other identities which involve attraction to more than one gender.

Bisexual identities: a brief history

It was not until the beginning of the 1970s that bisexuality began to emerge more prominently than in the past, as bisexual people began to find each other and form communities, particularly in major cities. This early bisexual movement took place amid the wider context of a cultural turn to free love and sexual liberation within Western culture (see Brennan & Hegarty, 2012; Donaldson, 1995; Udis-Kessler, 1995). Some researchers had previously included bisexuality within their wider studies of lesbian and gay identities, but by the mid-1970s, academics began to specifically focus on bisexuality as a distinct identity (see Brennan & Hegarty, 2012; Taylor, 2018). Others have thoroughly documented the history of academic writing on bisexuality (e.g., Angelides, 2001; Elia, Eliason, & Beemyn, 2018; Fox, 2004; Garber, 1995; Hemmings, 2002; Storr, 1999), and what follows is a brief overview to provide some context for the remainder of the book.

Early pioneering and influential contributors to the early literature included anthropologist Margaret Mead (1975), sociologists Philip Blumstein and Pepper Schwartz (1976a, 1976b, 1977), psychotherapist Charlotte Wolff (1977), and psychiatrist Fred/Fritz Klein (1978; Klein, Sepekoff, & Wolf, 1985). These people were the first to "break the silence" and write affirmatively about bisexual identities and the experiences of bisexual people (see Bowes-Catton, 2007; Brennan & Hegarty, 2012; Storr, 1999; Taylor, 2018, p. 104). Wolff's observation that "bisexuals are not only less conspicuous but more elusive than homosexuals" (Wolff, 1977, p. 67) captures a sense of the invisibility of bisexuality during this time. These writings were some of the first places in which bisexuality became visible and validated through the existence of these bisexual men and women's narratives.

During the 1980s, there was somewhat of a backwards step for lesbian and gay politics when the human immunodeficiency virus (HIV) was first identified and associated with same-sex behaviours between men. This was also a significant setback for bisexual people – men in particular – who were accused of spreading HIV from gay communities to heterosexual society (see Bowes-Catton, 2007; Taylor, 2018). Since the 1970s, bisexual women had been seen as traitors to the feminist cause within some lesbian communities (see Blumstein & Schwartz, 1976b, 1977; Rust, 1995). By the 1980s, bisexual people were also being seen as lacking commitment to the fight for lesbian and gay rights (e.g., Taylor, 2018; Udis-Kessler, 1995). It may partly have been a response to this negativity which mobilised bisexual groups and communities during this era (Taylor, 2018; Udis-Kessler, 1995).

The 1990s and 2000s saw a significant increase in bisexuality being discussed within the academy and the wider culture. From the early 1990s, books reported on the lives and identities of bisexual people, based on interviews or surveys with bisexual men and women (e.g., George, 1993; Klein & Schwartz, 2001; Orndorff, 1999; Weinberg, Williams, & Pryor, 1994). A number of anthologies were published, in which pertinent topics such as bisexual identities, relationships, lives, communities, and wider politics were discussed (e.g., Bisexual Anthology Collective, 1995; Firestein, 1996; Hutchins & Kaahumanu, 1991; The Off Pink Collective, 1996; Tucker, Highleyman, & Kaplan, 1995; Weise, 1992). During the 1990s and early 2000s, academics from various disciplinary backgrounds collated (and critically reviewed) the historical and contemporary literature on bisexuality and engaged in theoretical discussions of bisexual identities (e.g., Angelides, 2001; Firestein, 1996; Garber, 1995; Rust, 2000; Storr, 1999). A common theme was debates about where bisexuality might fit within, and contribute to, psychoanalysis, queer theory, and feminism (Angelides, 2001; Garber, 1995; Hemmings, 2002; Rust, 1995; The Off Pink Collective, 1996; Weise, 1992). In 2000, the *Journal of Bisexuality* was established, and this continues to provide a dedicated space where academics, activists, and allies can disseminate their research and writing. In the same year, Kenji Yoshino introduced the concept of "bisexual erasure" (Yoshino, 2000; Box 1.2).

BOX 1.2 KEY TERMS: BISEXUAL ERASURE

In 2000, law scholar Kenji Yoshino wrote about the social invisibility of bisexuality and introduced the concept of "bisexual erasure". He noted that bisexual invisibility falls under the invisibility of sexualities more broadly. He argued that there is a desire for sexuality to only be spoken of in euphemistic terms and discussed how same-sex desire is particularly unspeakable (e.g., in "don't ask, don't tell" military policies and "no promo homo" law statutes; Yoshino, 2000, p. 357). It is partly this which makes lesbian and gay identities – and bisexuality – invisible. He highlighted that bisexuality is also invisible in other ways, including when it is subsumed with lesbian and gay identities. Yoshino evidenced bisexual invisibility by documenting how infrequently bisexuality was mentioned in popular newspapers and academic publications in comparison with homosexuality. He drew on participant demographics from surveys of sexuality to evidence that there are as many bisexual people as there are lesbian and gay people. He argued that bisexual invisibility cannot therefore be a result of a lack of bisexual people.

Yoshino suggested that bisexuality poses a threat to the privileging of heterosexuality and the stability of sexuality (see also Ochs, 1996). He outlined three forms of bisexual erasure. The first is "class erasure", where the existence of bisexuality is denied in ways which link back to binary understandings (see Box 1.1). Bisexual people are assumed to be lesbian or gay but in denial, or heterosexual and seeking attention (see Chapter 3). The second is "individual erasure", where individuals who claim to be bisexual are erased through the suggestion that they are going through a temporary phase. The final form of erasure is "delegitimation", where bisexuality is acknowledged but stigmatised, hence bisexuality becomes visible but is rapidly erased as a valid form of sexuality (Yoshino, 2000; see also Chapter 3).

Since the mid-1990s and continuing to the present, there has been a considerable body of empirical research on biphobia and bisexual marginalisation, which is discussed in Chapter 3. From the early 2000s, there has also been a focus on bisexuality and mental health, with poor mental health among bisexual people discussed in relation to bisexual invisibility, marginalisation, and erasure (e.g., Eady, Dobinson, & Ross, 2011; Flanders, Dobinson, & Logie, 2015; Jorm, Korten, Rodgers, Jacomb, & Christensen, 2002; Mereish, Katz-Wise, & Woulfe, 2017; Ross, Dobinson, & Eady, 2010; for literature reviews, see Dodge & Sandfort, 2007; Feinstein & Dyar, 2017; Persson & Pfaus, 2015). Most recently, researchers have started to include, or specifically focus on, pansexual and asexual identities (e.g., Belous & Bauman, 2017; Bogaert, 2004; Borgogna, McDermott, Aita, & Kridel, 2018; Callis, 2014; Carrigan, 2011, 2016; Elizabeth, 2016; Flanders, LeBreton, Robinson, Bian, & Caravaca-Morera, 2017; Gonel, 2013; Morandini, Blaszczynski, & Dar-Nimrod, 2017; Sprott & Benoit Hadcock, 2018).

Defining bisexuality

Since bisexuality has been taken up as an identity, definitions have varied, with some researchers highlighting how difficult or elusive a satisfactory definition has been (e.g., Diamond, 2008; Firestein, 1996; Halperin, 2009; Hansen & Evans, 1985; Klein & Wolf, 1985; Rust, 1995; Swan, 2018a). Historically, bisexuality has been understood as a fixed third identity category (sometimes positioned at the midpoint between heterosexuality and homosexuality), involving attraction to, or behaviours with, men and women. Alternatively, it has been positioned as a fluid identity, which offers the capacity for identity not to be limited by gender, and to incorporate changes in attraction and behaviour over time and/or on a wide spectrum or continuum. Since the advent of queer theory, some have understood bisexuality as a revolutionary and radical position which holds the potential to break down all sexual and gender binaries and categories (see Angelides, 2001; Diamond, 2008; Firestein, 2007; Galupo, 2018; Garber, 1995; Hayfield, 2016; Hemmings, 2002).

Bisexuality has been operationalised in terms of attraction, behaviour, and self-identification, or as a combination of these (see Elia et al., 2018; Fox, 1996; Monro, 2015; Yoshino, 2000). In the late 1970s, Klein argued that there could be many dimensions to sexuality (Klein, 1978). He developed the Klein Sexual Orientation Grid (KSOG), with the aim of measuring identity as a "multi-variable process". The KSOG included seven distinct variables to be measured in "the past, present, and as an ideal". These were "attraction, behaviour, fantasy, social and emotional preference, self-identification and lifestyle" (Klein, 1978; 1980/2014; Klein et al., 1985, p. 38). This scale has been little utilised due to its complexity (Swan, 2018b). However, the notion of identity as based on thoughts, emotions, and perhaps most notably attraction, rather than behaviour, has commonly been incorporated in recent understandings (Harrad, 2016; Swan, 2018a). A recent study suggested that young people are likely to define their own bisexuality – and pansexuality – on the basis of attraction rather than on the basis of having necessarily engaged in sexual behaviours with anyone (Flanders et al., 2017).

Indeed, a common pattern in research has been the complexities of attraction, behaviour, and self-identification. Early researchers often identified that people's attractions and behaviours did not seem to distinctively relate to, or predict, how they identified their own sexuality (e.g., Blumstein & Schwartz, 1977; Rust, 1992, 1995; see also Bowes-Catton, 2007; Swan, 2018a). For example, Paula Rust (1995) identified that there were more commonalities between lesbian and bisexual women in their sexual attraction than there were differences (despite variations in their relationships). It has also been well documented that more people engage in sexual behaviours with more than one gender than identify as bisexual. This has implications in terms of healthcare and outreach, as well as in relation to the in/visibility of bisexuality (Swan, 2018a). Researchers have also noted that those using the same identity label are likely to have different definitions of what that means to them, and that how people name their own identities can change over time (e.g., Diamond, 2008; Halperin, 2009; Harrad, 2016; Orndorff, 1999; Rust, 1995; Swan, 2018a).

The limitations of the gender binary and the importance of the inclusion of trans people have been discussed by bisexual authors and activists and within bisexual communities (e.g., Firestein, 2007; Monro, 2015; Ochs, 1996, 2007). Some trans (including agender, genderfluid, genderqueer, and non-binary) people identify as bisexual and belong to bisexual communities (e.g., Barker, Bowes-Catton, Iantaffi, Cassidy, & Brewer, 2008; Dingle, 2016; Monro, 2015). Bisexual activists and academics have discussed how definitions of bisexuality have evolved alongside changing understandings of gender (Dingle, 2017; Eisner, 2013; Firestein, 2007; Hayfield & Lahti, 2017; Lapointe, 2017; Monro, 2015). The binary has been reconceptualised from attraction to "men/women" to attraction to those "like us/unlike us" or to "people with a similar gender to mine and people with a different gender to mine" (e.g., Fred, bisexual, trans, and genderqueer, in Dingle, 2016; see also, Dingle, 2017; Firestein, 2007). There has been some considerable focus, then, on patterns of attractions, behaviours, and relationships, and how best to understand bisexual identities. However, while there have been multiple models of sexuality, and a myriad of ways in which bisexuality might be defined, there is no singular definition. In this book, I use the definition of bisexuality which has been put forward by activist Robyn Ochs (2014):

the potential to be attracted, romantically and/or sexually, to people of more than one sex and/or gender, not necessarily at the same time, not necessarily in the same way, and not necessarily to the same degree.

I choose to use this definition for two key reasons. First, it is often utilised by bisexual organisations and has its roots within bisexual communities. Second, it captures a broad definition of bisexuality. It does so by acknowledging: (1) that bisexuality can be about romantic and/or sexual attraction (rather than being exclusively about sexual attraction or based only on behaviours); (2) that bisexual people can be attracted to people beyond the sex/gender binary; and (3) that their attractions to people of different sexes/genders may vary (e.g., bisexuality does not have to be 50/50 attraction and the extent of attractions to different genders may change according to time and context). This means that it is perhaps most likely to resonate for a broad range of people who identify as bisexual.

The emergence of pansexual, asexual, and other plurisexual identities

Overall, there has been an increase in people identifying as lesbian, gay, or bisexual (LGB). In 2012, 1.5% of the UK population over of the age of 16 were reported to identify as LGB, whereas by 2017 this figure had increased to 2% (Office for National Statistics, 2019). Additionally, surveys have reported that bisexual people make up the largest percentage of LGB people. According to one review of international surveys (from Australia, Canada, Norway, the UK, and the US), approximately 3.5% of the US adult population are LGB. Of these, 1.8% are bisexual, compared with 1.7% lesbian or gay (Gates, 2011). Over the last 10 years or so, there has been a significant increase in the numbers of young people in particular using newly emerging terms, such as pansexual, to capture their attractions to more than one gender, alongside an increasing recognition of a range of asexual identities (Belous & Bauman, 2017; Carrigan, 2011, 2016).

Defining pansexuality

The term pansexuality first came into use during the 1990s, alongside the less recognised pomosexuality (postmodern sexuality) (Belous & Bauman, 2017; Elizabeth, 2016; Lenius, 2001). Both terms were initially related to deconstructing traditional ideas about sexual desires, activities, and identities, and are likely to have been in response to queer theory. For some, queer and pansexual may be understood as overlapping terms, whereas by others they may be seen as distinct (Belous & Bauman, 2017; Elizabeth, 2016; Gonel, 2013). Early accounts of the term pansexual include its use within BDSM (bondage and discipline, dominance and submission, and sadism and masochism) communities. Pansexual could mean "it's okay for everyone to play with everyone else" (Lenius, 2001, p. 71), hence it referred to engaging in "non-normative" sexual behaviours. This included people who wanted to capture that their sexual activities – sometimes with people of varying genders – did not conform to traditional forms of heterosexuality (Elizabeth, 2016). More recently, although some participants have made links between BDSM/kink activities and their pansexuality (see Galupo, Henise, & Mercer, 2016; Sprott & Benoit Hadcock, 2018), definitions are rarely primarily related to BDSM. Within the context of what has been termed a "post-gay era", younger people are rejecting rigid definitions and categories of sexuality, while simultaneously using ever more nuanced and multiple terms to capture their own identities. For some, pansexuality is an anti-identity based on the deconstruction of sex, gender, and sexuality, and on resistance to all labels, particularly those which uphold binaries (e.g., Callis, 2014; Gonel, 2013; Morandini et al., 2017). The use of pansexuality may also be understood by some to reflect embracing fluidity, both in terms of changes in levels of attraction to people of various genders and in relation to changes in how any individual identifies their own gender over time (Elizabeth, 2016).

However, the meaning of pansexuality has perhaps predominantly come to refer to attraction to all genders across the gender spectrum, or "regardless of gender" (Elizabeth, 2016; Gonel, 2013, pp. 36–37). It has been argued by some that bisexuality deconstructs binary understandings of sexuality (homosexuality/heterosexuality), whereas pansexuality also explicitly deconstructs sex/gender binaries (male/man and female/woman) (Elizabeth, 2016). While pansexuality is sometimes conflated or used interchangeably with bisexuality, some have distinguished between bisexuality as binary and pansexual as non-binary (Belous & Bauman, 2017; see above for reconceptualisations of the bisexual binary). An increase in the visibility of trans identities, communities, activism, and movements may have informed the emergence and growing popularity of pansexuality (Elizabeth, 2016). Pansexuality may be used by anyone (e.g., people who are trans, genderqueer, genderfluid, and by cis people) who wants to explicitly acknowledge their awareness of gender on a spectrum and of their attractions to trans people (Elizabeth, 2016; Sprott & Benoit Hadcock, 2018). Some pansexual people and communities have used the term "hearts not parts" to succinctly capture the focus on people, rather than bodies and genitalia (e.g., participants in Galupo et al., 2016; Lapointe, 2017). However, this expression has been contested on some microblogging platforms such as Tumblr (for example, a search of "hearts not parts" brings up posts from contributors who argue that the term is problematic because it appears to erase the importance of gender for individuals and within Western societies, and that it is reductive in that it implies that for non-pansexual people, attraction is based purely on genitalia – whereas pansexual people could be interpreted as being positioned as somehow superior to others for their attractions being based on personality). Belous and Bauman (2017) analysed Internet sources and identified that pansexuality is often positioned as a response to tolerance and diversity, and as the new norm.

Defining asexuality and asexual spectrum identities

Since the early 2000s, there has also been a growth in awareness of the numbers of people identifying as asexual. This has partly been informed by the emergence of online and offline asexual communities and increased activism (Carrigan, 2016). An asexual person is commonly defined as someone "who does not experience sexual attraction" (Asexual Visibility and Education Network, n.d.; see also Carrigan, 2016). However, there is a great deal of diversity among those who identify as asexual or are part of asexual communities (Carrigan, 2011, 2016). Some have referred to these variations as "asexual spectrum" or "a-spec" identities (Pasquier, 2018). The terms demiromantic and demisexual refer to those who have the capacity to experience romantic or sexual attraction after a close emotional bond has been formed with someone (Asexuality Archive, n.d.; Asexual Visibility and Education Network, 2015; Pasquier, 2018). Greyromantic and grey-asexual are terms used by those who occasionally or infrequently experience romantic or sexual attraction (but do not necessarily require there to be an emotional bond), and who are therefore in "the 'grey area' between sexuality and asexuality" (Carrigan, 2015, p. 8; see also, Carrigan, 2011; Pasquier, 2018). Some people also use the terms aceflux and aroflux to capture that their romantic and sexual attractions fluctuate (Asexual Visibility and Education Network, 2015; Pasquier, 2018). Those who experience romantic and/or sexual attraction vary in terms of who they are romantically and/or sexually attracted to. Therefore, they may identify as heteroromantic, homoromantic, and, most relevant for this book, biromantic and/or panromantic, sometimes alongside grey-asexual or demisexual (Asexuality Archive, n.d.; Asexual Visibility and Education Network, 2015; Pasquier, 2018).

The in/visibility of identities

Key underpinnings of bisexual invisibility and erasure

Bisexual activists and their allies have noted some of the structural underpinnings of the invisibility and erasure of bisexuality. Bisexual invisibility and erasure (see Box 1.2) can be attributed to binary understandings of sexuality (see Box 1.1), where the world becomes understood as "consisting of heterosexual and homosexuals" and as a consequence bisexual people and their identities are absent or erased (Alarie & Gaudet, 2013, p. 200; Hartman, 2013; McLean, 2018). Dismissals of bisexuality which contribute to bisexual invisibility and erasure can also be attributed to monosexist and mononormative understandings of sexuality and relationships (Box 1.3).

BOX 1.3 KEY TERMS: MONOSEXUAL AND MONONORMA-TIVE UNDERSTANDINGS

Heterosexual, gay, and lesbian identities can all be referred to as monosexual. In heterosexuality, men are understood to only be attracted to women, and women to only be attracted to men. In homosexuality, men are understood to only be attracted to men, and women to only be attracted to women. The taken-for-granted assumption is that it is only possible to be attracted to – or have relationships with – people of one gender. Monosexism has been coined to refer to negativity towards people who do not comply with monosexuality (e.g., those who are attracted to more than one gender). The term mononormativity has been used in relation to identity and in relation to relationships. It can refer to cultural norms and values which assume that everyone is, or should be, monosexual. Monosexual and mononormative understandings of identities and relationships closely link with binary understandings of sexuality. Heterosexuality and homosexuality are valid within a mononormative framework, whereas bisexuality (and pansexuality, asexuality, and plurisexualities) are invalid. Mononormativity has also been used to refer to cultural norms and values which privilege monogamous relationships as normal and natural. Mononormativity therefore serves to validate monosexual people and monogamy and to vilify those who are attracted to more than one gender and/or engage in more than one relationship (e.g., Eisner, 2013, 2016; Ellis, Riggs, & Peel, 2020; Hemmings, 2002; Israel, 2018; McLean, 2018; Monro, 2015; Pieper & Bauer, 2006).

Bisexuality has also been appropriated by others in such a way that those who might be defined as bisexual are instead labelled as lesbian, or gay, or heterosexual, or with other identities (McLean, 2018). Present sexual behaviours, or the gender of a current partner, are often understood to determine sexuality. Therefore, the potential for identity to be based on attraction, or any consideration of past or potential future behaviours or relationships, is overlooked. The result is that those who are in long-term monogamous relationships are often assumed to be lesbian or gay – even when they continue to identify as bisexual. Therefore, bisexual people may only be considered "real bisexuals" by others when they are simultaneously sexually active and/or in relationships with people of more than one gender (Alarie & Gaudet, 2013; Hartman, 2013; McLean, 2018). In turn, this means that the assumption may be made that to be bisexual relies on being consensually non-monogamous/polyamorous (Robinson, 2013). Those who are polyamorous may also be understood in a range of additional negative ways (e.g., Grunt-Mejer & Campbell, 2016; Ritchie & Barker, 2006; Robinson, 2013; see also Chapter 3).

There are also other ways in which definitions of bisexuality are made so rigid that it is almost impossible for a "real bisexual" to exist. These include assumptions that to be bisexual means being equally attracted to men and women. Therefore, those whose attractions are not 50/50 may sometimes be understood by others as not "real bisexuals" (Alarie & Gaudet, 2013; McLean, 2018). These types of misnomer contribute to bisexual invisibility because restricting the meaning of bisexuality reduces the number of people considered to be "really bisexual" (see McLean, 2018; see also Chapter 3), despite the increasing numbers of people identifying with bisexuality (see above). Further, when bisexuality is understood within a set of rigid parameters, people may be less likely to identify as bisexual because their experience might not fit within such restrictive terms. It also means that those who do identify as bisexual may be less willing to disclose their bisexuality to others due to fears of dismissal. These factors all further contribute to bisexual invisibility and erasure (Alarie & Gaudet, 2013; McLean, 2018; see also Chapters 4 and 5). Another key factor in bisexual invisibility is the amalgamation of bisexual people with lesbian and/or gay people within acronyms/initialisms, communities, and academic research (Barker et al., 2008; McLean, 2018; see also Chapter 5).

The erasure of bisexuality, pansexuality, asexuality, and plurisexual identities under the LGBTQ+ umbrella

During the 1960s, the word gay came into popular usage as an umbrella term, before lesbians began to specifically be mentioned (e.g., gay men and lesbian women) (Iovannone, 2018). Since the early 1990s, the initialism LGBT (lesbian, gay, bisexual, and trans) came into popular usage, and this inclusion of bisexual and trans was seen as cause for celebration (Firestein, 1996; Iovannone, 2018). In more recent years, efforts to ensure that collective terms are inclusive of a wider range of identities have led to adaptations and extensions of LGBT initialisms and acronyms (Iovannone, 2018). However, there is little evidence that these initialisms and acronyms are as coherent and inclusive of multiple identities as the terms might imply (Clarke & Peel, 2007; Clarke & Rúdólfsdóttir, 2005; Elia et al., 2018). Instead, the inclusion of B for bisexual is rarely meaningful and instead is often in name only (Elia, 2010; McLean, 2018). The "plight of the alphabet soup approach to inclusion" (Elia, 2010, p. 457) is that bisexuality, and other identities, are effectively erased:

> Anyone who is even remotely familiar with the literature has seen the LGBT moniker, which has expanded over the years to include LG*Bisexual*TQQI (lesbian, gay, bisexual, transgender, queer, questioning, and intersex). For all intents and purposes, it is an empty *B*. It has been a placeholder for bisexuality/bisexuals in the string of letters that are reserved for sexual and gendered others.
>
> *(Elia, 2010, p. 457)*

While the LGBTQ+ initialism is sometimes extended to include asexuality (e.g., LGBTQIA: lesbian, gay, bisexual, trans, queer, intersex, and asexual), to date this is considerably limited. P for pansexuality is sometimes considered to be subsumed within the plus symbol in LGBTQ+, but often remains unacknowledged. Recently, LGBTQQIP2SAA (lesbian, gay, bisexual, trans, queer, questioning, intersex, pansexual, two spirit, asexual, and ally) and QUILTBAG (e.g., variations of queer and/or questioning, undecided, intersex, lesbian, trans and two spirit, bisexual, asexual/ally, gay, and genderqueer) have come into existence. However, LGBT and LGBTQ+ remain the dominant initialisms.

The bisexual umbrella

As an array of terms referring to attractions to multiple genders have come into usage, the word bisexual has sometimes been used as an umbrella term (Eisner, 2013; see also Belous & Bauman, 2017; Flanders, 2017; Galupo, 2018; Lapointe, 2017). The "bi-spectrum" identities listed under the "bisexual umbrella" (Eisner, 2011, 2013, p. 28; also see *The Bisexual Umbrella* on the e-resources tab of this book's Routledge webpage) vary across different versions, but have included:

- Biromantic/panromantic: terms used by those who experience romantic attraction to capture the genders of those they are romantically attracted to (also see above for a discussion of other a-spec identities).
- Fluid: a term used to indicate fluidity in the genders one is attracted to, or to fluidity in the extent of attraction to different genders, or to capture (the possibility) that the genders of those to whom one is attracted might change over time (Brown & Lilton, 2019; Eisner, 2013).
- Omnisexual: a term used by those who are attracted to people of all genders across the gender spectrum; the term may be used interchangeably with pansexual by some people (Eisner, 2013; Okoli, Odumodu, Eze, & Emma-Echiegu, 2017).
- Pansexual: a term to indicate attraction to all genders across the gender spectrum or "regardless of gender" (Elizabeth, 2016; Gonel, 2013, pp. 36–37; also see above).
- Plurisexual: used by some individuals as their preferred term to capture their attraction to more than one gender; more commonly used to collectively refer to anyone who is attracted to more than one or multiple genders (Brown & Lilton, 2019).
- Polysexual: a term to refer to attraction to many, but not necessarily all, genders (Eisner, 2013; Gray & Moore, 2018); sometimes used as an umbrella term referring to attraction to many genders, in contrast to monosexual (see Box 1.3) (Gonel, 2013).
- Queer: a term that has been used in a range of ways, including to indicate a rejection of all identities by both those attracted to one gender and those attracted to multiple genders; as a collective term for the wider LGBT+ community; and to refer to attraction to more than one gender (e.g., Eisner, 2013; Galupo, 2018).
- Sapiosexual: a term referring to attraction based on intelligence, regardless of gender (Israel, 2018); the term has recently been discussed in the mainstream mass media in response to French equalities minister Marlène Schiappa publicly identifying as sapiosexual (e.g., Sage, 2019).

Some have spoken of the bisexual umbrella (and the similar trans umbrella; see Davidson, 2007) as being a way to metaphorically gather together, to examine common experience, and to work together in solidarity towards shared goals

(Eisner, 2013; Flanders, 2017; Galupo, 2018). This may seem an appealing option, particularly given that many might identify with multiple terms under the umbrella (e.g., as pansexual and bisexual; see Flanders et al., 2017; Lapointe, 2017), and are likely to have some similar experiences (Flanders, 2017). Some have argued that because definitions of pansexuality are sometimes understood to be broader than definitions of bisexuality, it may actually be more appropriate to consider pansexual the all-encompassing umbrella term (Belous & Bauman, 2017). Further, those who are bisexual, pansexual, and queer (and who identify with other terms) may describe their sexualities in ways which are both similar to and different from each other (Flanders, 2017; Galupo, 2018). Similarly, while those who identify with these different identities may share commonalities, so too may their experiences be distinctive (Flanders, 2017; Persson & Pfaus, 2015; Swan, 2018a). Therefore, researchers have argued that subsuming multiple terms may be inappropriate, because it blurs the boundaries between them, which potentially obscures important differences (e.g., of stigmatisation; see Flanders et al., 2017; Persson & Pfaus, 2015). The umbrella can also be problematic because it renders bisexuality invisible through its amalgamation with other identities and risks making the other identities included under the umbrella equally invisible, as they too become subsumed (Swan, 2018a). Therefore, the bisexual umbrella may be problematic for inclusion/exclusion and similarities/differences in similar ways to the LGBTQ+ umbrella.

When discussing the bisexual umbrella, Eisner (2013) emphasises that only those who want to be included under it should be so. However, researchers (and others) may subsume (variations of) multiple identities under the umbrella without participants' permission. While this may be for pragmatic reasons (e.g., sample size; see Flanders et al., 2017), nonetheless this takes away that agency. Therefore, in fitting with Eisner's recommendation it would be advisable not to subsume multiple identities without participants' permission, and to take into consideration the complexities and controversies discussed above when considering collecting together multiple identities into a singular category for research purposes. Nonetheless, there may be benefits in coming together in certain circumstances and working collectively for the purposes of activism and advocacy (Eisner, 2013; Flanders, 2017).

A specific and pertinent example of invisibility: Bisexuality, pansexuality, asexuality, and plurisexual identities within academic publications

Despite a significant increase in studies of bisexuality, there remains a relative lack of meaningful inclusion of bisexuality within academic research and writing. This in itself serves as an example of the erasure and invisibility of bisexuality which also extends to pansexuality, asexuality, and plurisexualities. A number of authors have written about the overlooking of some or all of these identities within psychology textbooks, psychological literature, and wider academic discourse (e.g., Barker, 2007; Brown & Lilton, 2019; Elia et al., 2018; Ferguson & Gilmour, 2018; Gray & Moore, 2018; Monro, Hines, & Osborne, 2017; Petford, 2003). For example, psychologist Meg-John Barker's (2007) analysis of 22 undergraduate psychology textbooks identified that around half did not mention bisexuality. Instead, they mainly presented sexuality as primarily heterosexual, with some limited acknowledgement of lesbian and gay sexualities. These bestselling introductory, biological, developmental, and social psychological texts often only included definitions or mentions of bisexuality early on in the book before omitting it in the remainder of the text. Barker highlights that the lack of meaningful coverage of bisexuality is anti-bisexual and risks perpetuating the invisibility of bisexuality and myths about bisexual people. They argue that the exclusion of bisexuality in textbooks reflects binary understandings of gender and sexuality (see Box 1.1).

It is worth noting that some specialist textbooks which are specifically focused on LBGTQ+ sexualities have made considerable efforts to be meaningfully inclusive of bisexuality (e.g., Clarke & Peel, 2007; Ellis et al., 2020). Nonetheless, even some specialist sexualities books seemingly remain limited in scope. For example, in a recent analysis of bisexual content in books on sexualities within sociology and political sciences, Monro et al. (2017) identify similar issues to Barker (2007). First, bisexuality is often invisible through minimal inclusion within, or total exclusion from, books' indexes. Second, when bisexuality is included, there is less coverage of bisexuality than of lesbian and gay identities. Further, bisexuality is often marginalised and misrepresented in ways which are othering. The paper highlights that same-sex sexualities also have a history of being erased but that lesbian and gay studies have become somewhat more established than bisexual studies, perhaps because bisexual identities developed later than lesbian and gay identities (Monro et al., 2017).

This lack of representation is not limited to sociology and political sciences, nor to books, nor to bisexuality. Ferguson and Gilmour (2018) analysed the content of peer-reviewed empirical papers published within US social work journals between 2008 and 2016. In their literature search, they included a range of plurisexual identity terms (e.g., asexual, bisexual, demisexual, non-monosexual, omnisexual, pansexual, polysexual, queer). While they found a total of 677 papers, after they applied various criteria, just four articles of relevance remained. Their criteria required that the papers were relevant "qualitative and/or quantitative" empirical studies which included US plurisexual participants – rather than research which consisted of secondary analysis, or publications in other formats (such as book reviews or commentaries), or research which only included participants with "monosex identities" (p. 27). In their content analysis, the authors identified that there was minimal focus on specific identities; instead, all forms of plurisexualities were amalgamated with lesbian and gay identities (Ferguson & Gilmour, 2018). This amalgamation is a key factor which contributes to a lack of understanding and perpetuates the erasure and invisibility of bisexuality and other identities which relate to attraction to more than one gender.

Introducing the troublesome topic of terminology

In this book, I aim to be inclusive of bisexual, pansexual, and asexual/aromantic people, as well as those who use other terms to define their attractions to multiple genders (such as those listed above). Many of the topics and ideas discussed in each of the forthcoming chapters may relate to some or all of these identities. However, there are likely to also be nuances in relation to specific identities, and more research is needed to establish whether, and in what ways, this is the case. In the main, I list bisexual, pansexual, and asexual identities in order of the prominence of research available about them. Some people use both bisexual and pansexual to define their identities (or indeed use other multiple terms) and the implications of this are discussed in Chapter 6. For this reason, it is difficult to know in what ways pansexual people's identities, experiences, and lives might be distinct from those of bisexual people – and in what ways they might overlap. There is minimal research on those who define as pansexual, omnisexual, and with other identities, and that which exists often amalgamates these identities with bisexuality and/or with each other. Similarly, the extant research rarely distinguishes between asexuality and a-spec identities. Therefore, the research included in this book is that which has broadly reported findings about asexuality and asexual people. It may be the case that these studies did (or did not) include a-spec identities such as biromantic/panromantic. Similarly, studies with bisexual and pansexual people may (or may not) have included people who also identified with a-spec identities, such as biromantic and panromantic. While it is not my ideal scenario to use an umbrella term for all the reasons I discussed above, I do nonetheless include the term plurisexualities to capture additional identities relating to attraction to multiple genders. In doing so, I aim to acknowledge the existence of these identities, despite how little research has specifically focused on each of them (which makes discussing them individually unfeasible). It is not my intention to suggest that these identities can or should be conflated, but to draw attention to their existence and the possibility of some findings potentially also relating to them.

I use the term trans to refer to those who are transgender, agender, genderfluid, genderqueer, non-binary, and who affiliate with any other form of trans identities. I do so to situate gender as potentially transitionary and to ensure that the term is sufficiently open to capture difference, diversity, complexity, and uncertainty (see Halberstam, 2018). Finally, the use of the term homosexual has come to be associated with the pathologisation of those attracted to people of the same sex/gender. For this reason, the preferred terms in this book are lesbian and gay, or same-sex/gender sexualities, unless used in a historical context or when reporting others' terminology.

Introducing the content of this book

The focus of this book is on in/visibility. I am by far not the first to argue that bisexuality is invisible. As discussed above, since the 1990s a number of bisexual and bisexual-affirmative authors have noted that bisexuality and bisexual people have been silenced, dismissed, and erased, and have therefore been invisible. Nonetheless, the in/visibility of bisexuality – and of pansexuality, asexuality, and plurisexualities – remains a pertinent issue. Bisexual erasure has an entry on Wikipedia, bisexual invisibility has been discussed in *The Huffington Post*, and other sites within and outside academia have also focused on the implications of invisibility and erasure for bisexual people. In this book, I explore some examples of the ways in which bisexuality remains invisible, and discuss the impact of invisibility and invalidation. As a psychologist, I do primarily focus on psychological publications, but I also refer to research from other social science disciplines.

Chapter 2 offers an insight into the historical underpinnings of bisexual invisibility and erasure, through an exploration of how first-wave and second-wave sexologists conceptualised bisexuality. The chapter evidences how early sexologists' understandings of sexuality provided the foundations of binary understandings of sexuality as they grappled to make attractions to more than one gender fit with their theoretical ideas. Some second-wave sexologists (with the notable exception of Kinsey) tended to entirely overlook bisexuality, and therefore also contributed to the erasure and invisibility of bisexual people and their identities.

The focus of Chapter 3 is on marginalisation. When bisexuality has become visible it has often been denigrated and dismissed. While bisexual, pansexual, asexual, and plurisexual people are often overlooked within academic research – which in itself contributes to the invisibility of these identities – there is a relatively large body of research on bisexual marginalisation. This chapter discusses research methods and focuses on how, when bisexuality and other identities become visible, they are often rapidly invalidated. There is evidence to indicate that this has implications for bisexual people and these may extend to those who are pansexual, asexual, and plurisexual.

Chapter 4 introduces the notion of visual identity. An individual's appearance can be understood as one way in which our identities can become visible. While lesbian and gay communities have a long history of becoming visible through dress and appearance, this is seemingly not the case for bisexual, pansexual, asexual, or plurisexual people. This means that they may be invisible to each other and to wider audiences.

Chapters 3 and 4 include quotations from bisexual women who participated in research exploring bisexual appearance and visual identity, and bisexual marginalisation. It seems sensible to introduce them here. These 20 self-identified bisexual women were recruited via calls for participants in a local free community newspaper and an advert in *Bi Community News*, through flyers handed out at bisexual community events, and via snowball sampling. They were mainly White, middle-class, well-educated, and in relationships (six with a woman; nine with a man; three had more than one partner or were consensually non-monogamous/polyamorous) with an age range of 19–53 years (with a mean age of 33 years). Most had some past or present experience of bisexual communities. Their data is used to illustrate particular points within these chapters.

In Chapter 5, the cultural invisibility of bisexuality, pansexuality, asexuality, and other plurisexual identities in education, employment, and (mainly mainstream) mass media is discussed. The invisibility and invalidation of bisexuality, pansexuality, asexuality, and other plurisexualities in schools, workplaces, and the media contribute to the erasure and dismissal of these identities. In turn, this impacts on bisexual, pansexual, asexual, and plurisexual people's experiences and lives.

Finally, Chapter 6 focuses on the ways in which bisexual, pansexual, asexual, and plurisexual people and their identities have become somewhat more visible than they were in the past. This increased visibility has taken considerable effort, and remains somewhat limited. I end by drawing some conclusions about in/visibility. I conclude that bisexual, pansexual, asexual, and plurisexual people and their identities remain largely invisible to each other, to others, and within the wider culture. There have been considerable efforts by individuals, activists, academics, and organisations to raise the visibility of bisexuality in particular – with more recent attempts to include pansexuality and other plurisexual identities. Asexual communities have also been growing in recent years and therefore asexuality too has become somewhat more visible. Visibility can be an important strategy for creating a sense of shared identity and collective community, and for enabling advocacy and education. However, the risk of visibility is that it can lead to further invalidation when sexualities are perceived as a threat. In more recent years, while there has been an increased acceptance and somewhat more visibility of bisexuality, this remains limited and bisexual people continue to be marginalised. This marginalisation has important implications for bisexual people and feeds into further erasure and invisibility through the dismissal of bisexuality as a valid identity. More recently there is some evidence that pansexual, asexual, and plurisexual people may find that their identities are also subject to issues of invisibility and invalidation. It would seem that becoming visible and validated is challenging for all identities which fall outside the sex/gender binary. While visibility will not necessarily lead to validation, nonetheless when bisexuality, pansexualities, asexualities, and plurisexualities do become more visible there is scope for raising awareness of these identities and therefore of them becoming better recognised, represented, and understood by others within the wider culture.

References

Alarie, M., & Gaudet, S. (2013). "I don't know if she is bisexual or if she just wants to get attention": Analyzing the various mechanisms through which emerging adults invisibilize bisexuality. *Journal of Bisexuality*, *13*(2), 191–214. doi:10.1080/15299716.2013.780004

Angelides, S. (2001). *A history of bisexuality*. Chicago: University of Chicago Press.

Asexual Visibility and Education Network. (2015, May 24). A list of romantic orientations. Retrieved from www.asexuality.org/en/topic/119238-a-list-of-romantic-orientations/

Asexual Visibility and Education Network. (n.d.). Welcome. Retrieved from www.asexuality.org/

Asexuality Archive. (n.d.). Glossary. Retrieved from www.asexualityarchive.com/glossary/

Barker, M. (2007). Heteronormativity and the exclusion of bisexuality in psychology. In V. Clarke, & E. Peel (Eds.), *Out in psychology: Lesbian, gay, bisexual, trans, and queer perspectives* (pp. 86–118). Chichester: John Wiley & Sons.

Barker, M., Bowes-Catton, H., Iantaffi, A., Cassidy, A., & Brewer, L. (2008). British bisexuality: A snapshot of bisexual representations and identities in the United Kingdom. *Journal of Bisexuality, 8*(1–2), 141–162. doi:10.1080/15299710802143026

Belous, C. K., & Bauman, M. L. (2017). What's in a name? Exploring pansexuality online. *Journal of Bisexuality, 17*(1), 58–72. doi:10.1080/15299716.2016.1224212

Bisexual Anthology Collective. (Eds.). (1995). *Plural desires: Writing bisexual women's realities.* Toronto: Sister Vision: Black Women and Women of Colour Press.

Blumstein, P. W., & Schwartz, P. (1976a). Bisexuality in men. *Urban Life, 5*(3), 339–358. doi:10.1177/089124167600500305

Blumstein, P. W., & Schwartz, P. (1976b). Bisexuality in women. *Archives of Sexual Behavior, 5*(2), 171–181. doi:10.1007/BF01541873

Blumstein, P. W., & Schwartz, P. (1977). Bisexuality: Some social psychological issues. *Journal of Social Issues, 33*(2), 30–45. doi:10.1111/j.1540-4560.1977.tb02004.x

Bogaert, A. F. (2004). Asexuality: Prevalence and associated factors in a national probability sample. *Journal of Sex Research, 41*(3), 279–287. doi:10.1080/00224490409552235

Borgogna, N. C., McDermott, R. C., Aita, S. L., & Kridel, M. M. (2018). Anxiety and depression across gender and sexual minorities: Implications for transgender, gender nonconforming, pansexual, demisexual, asexual, queer, and questioning individuals. *Psychology of Sexual Orientation and Gender Diversity, 6*(1), 54–63. doi:10.1037/sgd0000306

Bowes-Catton, H. (2007). Resisting the binary: Discourses of identity and diversity in bisexual politics 1988–1996. *Lesbian and Gay Psychology Review, 8*(1), 58–70.

Brennan, T., & Hegarty, P. (2012). Charlotte Wolff's contribution to bisexual history and to (sexuality) theory and research: A reappraisal for queer times. *Journal of the History of Sexuality, 21*(1), 141–161. doi:10.1353/sex.2012.0010

Brown, M. F., & Lilton, D. L. (2019). Finding the "B" in LGBTQ+: Collections and practices that support the bisexual and pansexual communities. In B. Mehra (Ed.), *LGBTQ+ librarianship in the 21st century: Emerging directions of advocacy and community engagement in diverse information environments* (pp. 143–165). Bingley: Emerald. doi:10.1108/S0065-283020190000045013

Butler, J. (1990/2006). *Gender trouble: Feminism and the subversion of identity.* New York: Routledge.

Callis, A. S. (2014). Bisexual, pansexual, queer: Non-binary identities and the sexual borderlands. *Sexualities, 17*(1–2), 63–80. doi:10.1177/1363460713511094

Capulet, I. (2010). With reps like these: Bisexuality and celebrity status. *Journal of Bisexuality, 10*(3), 294–308. doi:10.1080/15299716.2010.500962

Carrigan, M. (2011). There's more to life than sex? Difference and commonality within the asexual community. *Sexualities, 14*(4), 462–478. doi:10.1177/1363460711406462

Carrigan, M. (2015). Asexuality. In C. Richards, & M. J. Barker (Eds.), The Palgrave handbook of sexuality and gender (pp. 7–23). Basingstoke: Palgrave Macmillan. doi:10.1057/9781137345899_2

Carrigan, M. (2016). Asexuality. In A. E. Goldberg (Ed.), *The Sage encyclopedia of LGBTQ studies* (pp. 92–94). London: Sage.

Clarke, V., & Peel, E. (2007). From lesbian and gay psychology to LGBTQ psychologies: A journey into the unknown (or unknowable)? In V. Clarke, & E. Peel (Eds.), *Out in psychology: Lesbian, gay, bisexual, trans and queer perspectives* (pp. 11–35). Chichester: John Wiley & Sons. doi:10.1002/9780470713099.ch2

Clarke, V., & Rúdólfsdóttir, A. G. (2005). Love conquers all? An exploration of guidance books for family and friends of lesbians and gay men. *Psychology of Women Section Review*, 7(2), 37–48.

Davidson, M. (2007). Seeking refuge under the umbrella: Inclusion, exclusion, and organizing within the category transgender. *Sexuality Research & Social Policy*, 4(4), 60–80. doi:10.1525/srsp.2007.4.4.60

Diamond, L. M. (2008). Female bisexuality from adolescence to adulthood: Results from a 10-year longitudinal study. *Developmental Psychology*, 44(1), 5–14. doi:10.1037/0012-1649.44.1.5

Dingle, C. (2016, February 22). "We're just not hung up about gender": Bisexuality & binary/non-binary relationships. Retrieved from www.thisisbiscuit.co.uk/were-just-not-hung-up-about-gender-bisexuality-binarynon-binary-relationships/

Dingle, C. (2017, April 18). Pansexuality vs. bisexuality: The big debate: Does "bi" really mean an attraction to just two genders and "pan" an attraction to all genders? Retrieved from www.curvemag.com/Pansexuality-VS-Bisexuality-The-Big-Debate-1835/

Dodge, B., & Sandfort, T. G. M. (2007). A review of mental health research on bisexual individuals when compared to homosexual and heterosexual individuals. In B. A. Firestein (Ed.), *Becoming visible: Counseling bisexuals across the lifespan* (pp. 28–51). London: Sage.

Donaldson, S. (1995). The bisexual movement's beginnings in the 1970s: A personal retrospective. In N. Tucker, L. Highleyman, & R. Kaplan (Eds.), *Bisexual politics: Theories, queries & visions* (pp. 31–45). Binghamton: Haworth Press.

Eady, A., Dobinson, C., & Ross, L. E. (2011). Bisexual people's experiences with mental health services: A qualitative investigation. *Community Mental Health Journal*, 47(4), 378–389. doi:10.1007/s10597-010-9329-x

Eisner, S. (2011, November 23). The bisexual umbrella. Retrieved from https://radicalbi.wordpress.com/2011/11/23/the-bisexual-umbrella/

Eisner, S. (2013). *Bi: Notes for a bisexual revolution.* Berkeley: Seal Press.

Eisner, S. (2016). Monosexism. In A. E. Goldberg (Ed.), *The Sage encyclopedia of LGBTQ studies* (pp. 793–796). London: Sage.

Elia, J., Eliason, M., & Beemyn, G. (2018). Mapping bisexual studies: Past and present, and implications for the future. In D. J. Swan, & S. Habibi (Eds.), *Bisexuality: Theories, research, and recommendations for the invisible sexuality* (pp. 1–18). Cham: Springer. doi:10.1007%2F978-3-319-71535-3_1

Elia, J. P. (2010). Bisexuality and school culture: School as a prime site for bi-intervention. *Journal of Bisexuality*, 10(4), 452–471. doi:10.1080/15299716.2010.521060

Elizabeth, A. (2016). Pansexuality. In A. E. Goldberg (Ed.), *The Sage encyclopedia of LGBTQ studies* (pp. 833–835). London: Sage.

Ellis, S. J., Riggs, D. W., & Peel, E. (2020). *Lesbian, gay, bisexual, trans, intersex, and queer psychology: An introduction* (2nd ed.). Cambridge: Cambridge University Press. doi:10.1017/9781108303750

Feinstein, B. A., & Dyar, C. (2017). Bisexuality, minority stress, and health. *Current Sexual Health Reports*, 9(1), 42–49. doi:10.1007/s11930-017-0096-3

Ferguson, A., & Gilmour, M. (2018). Non-monosex research publication in US-based social work journals between 2008–2016. *Journal of Evidence-Informed Social Work*, 15(1), 23–37. doi:10.1080/23761407.2017.1391730

Firestein, B. A. (1996). *Bisexuality: The psychology and politics of an invisible minority.* London: Sage.

Firestein, B. A. (2007). *Becoming visible: Counseling bisexuals across the lifespan.* Chichester: Columbia University Press.

Flanders, C. E. (2017). Under the bisexual umbrella: Diversity of identity and experience. *Journal of Bisexuality*, *17*(1), 1–6.

Flanders, C. E., Dobinson, C., & Logie, C. (2015). "I'm never really my full self": Young bisexual women's perceptions of their mental health. *Journal of Bisexuality*, *15*(4), 454–480. doi:10.1080/15299716.2015.1079288

Flanders, C. E., LeBreton, M. E., Robinson, M., Bian, J., & Caravaca-Morera, J. A. (2017). Defining bisexuality: Young bisexual and pansexual people's voices. *Journal of Bisexuality*, *17*(1), 39–57. doi:10.1080/15299716.2016.1227016

Fox, R. C. (1996). Bisexuality in perspective: A review of theory and research. In B. A. Firestein (Ed.), *Bisexuality: The psychology and politics of an invisible minority* (pp. 3–50). London: Sage.

Fox, R. C. (2004). Bisexuality: A reader's guide to the social science literature. *Journal of Bisexuality*, *4*(1–2), 161–255. doi:10.1300/J159v04n01_12

Galupo, M. P. (2018). Plurisexual identity labels and the marking of bisexual desire. In D. J. Swan, & S. Habibi (Eds.), *Bisexuality: Theories, research, and recommendations for the invisible sexuality* (pp. 61–75). Cham: Springer. doi:10.1007/978-3-319-71535-3_4

Galupo, M. P., Henise, S. B., & Mercer, N. L. (2016). "The labels don't work very well": Transgender individuals' conceptualizations of sexual orientation and sexual identity. *International Journal of Transgenderism*, *17*(2), 93–104. doi:10.1080/15532739.2016.1189373

Garber, M. (1995). *Vice versa: Bisexuality and the eroticism of everyday life*. New York: Simon & Schuster.

Gates, G. J. (2011). *How many people are lesbian, gay, bisexual, and transgender?* Los Angeles: Williams Institute. Retrieved from https://williamsinstitute.law.ucla.edu/wp-content/uploads/Gates-How-Many-People-LGBT-Apr-2011.pdf

George, S. (1993). *Women and bisexuality*. London: Scarlet Press.

Gonel, A. H. (2013). Pansexual identification in online communities: Employing a collaborative queer method to study pansexuality. *Graduate Journal of Social Science*, *10*(1), 36–59.

Gray, A. L., & Moore, E. W. (2018). Understanding the relationship between sexual identity, life satisfaction, psychological well-being, and online community use. *Modern Psychological Studies*, *23*(2), 1–25.

Grunt-Mejer, K., & Campbell, C. (2016). Around consensual nonmonogamies: Assessing attitudes toward nonexclusive relationships. *The Journal of Sex Research*, *53*(1), 45–53. doi:10.1080/00224499.2015.1010193

Halberstam, J. (2018). *Trans*: A quick and quirky account of gender variability*. Oakland: University of California Press. doi:10.1525/9780520966109

Halperin, D. M. (2009). Thirteen ways of looking at a bisexual. *Journal of Bisexuality*, *9*(3–4), 451–455. doi:10.1080/15299710903316679

Hansen, C. E., & Evans, A. (1985). Bisexuality reconsidered: An idea in pursuit of a definition. *Journal of Homosexuality*, *11*(1–2), 1–6. doi:10.1300/J082v11n01_01

Harrad, K. (2016). The basics. In K. Harrad (Ed.), *Purple prose: Bisexuality in Britain* (pp. 3–18). Portland: Thorntree Press.

Hartman, J. E. (2013). Creating a bisexual display: Making bisexuality visible. *Journal of Bisexuality*, *13*(1), 39–62. doi:10.1080/15299716.2013.755727

Hayfield, N. (2016). Bisexualities. In A. E. Goldberg (Ed.), *The Sage encyclopedia of LGBTQ studies* (pp. 128–131). London: Sage.

Hayfield, N., & Lahti, A. (2017). Reflecting on bisexual identities and relationships: Nikki Hayfield in conversation with Annukka Lahti. *Psychology of Sexualities Review*, *8*(2), 68–75.

Hemmings, C. (2002). *Bisexual spaces: A geography of sexuality and gender.* London: Routledge.

Hutchins, L., & Kaahumanu, L. (Eds.). (1991). *Bi any other name: Bisexual people speak out.* Los Angeles: Alyson Books.

Iovannone, J. J. (2018, June 9). A brief history of the LGBTQ initialism: How did the LGBTQ community come to be known as such? Retrieved from https://medium.com/queer-history-for-the-people/a-brief-history-of-the-lgbtq-initialism-e89db1cf06e3

Israel, T. (2018). Bisexuality: From margin to center. *Psychology of Sexual Orientation and Gender Diversity, 5*(2), 233–242. doi:10.1037/sgd0000294

Jorm, A. F., Korten, A. E., Rodgers, B., Jacomb, P. A., & Christensen, H. (2002). Sexual orientation and mental health: Results from a community survey of young and middle-aged adults. *British Journal of Psychiatry, 180*(5), 423–427. doi:10.1192/bjp.180.5.423

Kinsey, A. C., Pomeroy, B. P., & Martin, C. E. (1948). *Sexual behaviour in the human male.* London: W. B. Saunders.

Kinsey, A. C., Pomeroy, B. P., Martin, C. E., & Gebhard, P. H. (1953). *Sexual behaviour in the human female.* London: W. B. Saunders.

Klein, F. (1978). *The bisexual option.* New York: Arbor House.

Klein, F. (1980/2014). Are you sure you're heterosexual? Or homosexual? Or even bisexual? *Journal of Bisexuality, 14*(3–4), 341–346. doi:10.1080/15299716.2014.953282

Klein, F., & Schwartz, T. (2001). *Bisexual and gay husbands, their stories, their words.* New York: Harrington Park Press.

Klein, F., Sepekoff, B., & Wolf, T. J. (1985). Sexual orientation: A multi-variable dynamic process. *Journal of Homosexuality, 11*(1), 35–49. doi:10.1300/J082v11n01_04

Klein, F., & Wolf, T. J. (Eds.). (1985). *Two lives to lead: Bisexuality in men and women.* New York: Harrington Park Press.

Lapointe, A. A. (2017). "It's not pans, it's people": Student and teacher perspectives on bisexuality and pansexuality. *Journal of Bisexuality, 17*(1), 88–107. doi:10.1080/15299716.2016.1196157

Lenius, S. (2001). Bisexuals and BDSM: Bisexual people in a pansexual community. *Journal of Bisexuality, 1*(4), 69–78. doi:10.1300/J159v01n04_06

McLean, K. (2008). Silences and stereotypes: The impact of (mis)constructions of bisexuality on Australian bisexual men and women. *Gay & Lesbian Issues and Psychology Review, 4*(3), 158–165.

McLean, K. (2018). Bisexuality in society. In D. J. Swan, & S. Habibi (Eds.), *Bisexuality: Theories, research, and recommendations for the invisible sexuality* (pp. 77–93). Cham: Springer. doi:10.1007/978-3-319-71535-3_5

Mead, M. (1975). Bisexuality: What's it all about? *Redbook,* January, 29–31.

Mereish, E. H., Katz-Wise, S. L., & Woulfe, J. (2017). Bisexual-specific minority stressors, psychological distress, and suicidality in bisexual individuals: The mediating role of loneliness. *Prevention Science, 18*(6), 716–725. doi:10.1007/s11121-017-0804 2

Monro, S. (2015). *Bisexuality: Identities, politics, and theories.* Basingstoke: Palgrave Macmillan.

Monro, S., Hines, S., & Osborne, A. (2017). Is bisexuality invisible? A review of sexualities scholarship 1970–2015. *Sociological Review, 65*(4), 663–681. doi:10.1177/0038026117695488

Morandini, J. S., Blaszczynski, A., & Dar-Nimrod, I. (2017). Who adopts queer and pansexual sexual identities? *Journal of Sex Research, 54*(7), 911–922. doi:10.1080/00224499.2016.1249332

Ochs, R. (1996). Biphobia: It goes more than two ways. In B. A. Firestein (Ed.), *Bisexuality: The psychology and politics of an invisible minority* (pp. 217–239). London: Sage.

Ochs, R. (2007). What's in a name? In B. In A. Firestein (Ed.), *Becoming visible: Counseling bisexuals across the lifespan* (pp. 72–86). London: Sage.

Ochs, R. (2014, September 14). *Understanding bisexuality: Challenging stigma, reducing disparities, and caring for patients.* National LGBT Health Education Center. Retrieved from www.lgbthealtheducation.org/wp-content/uploads/Understanding-Bisexuality-Final.pdf

Rose, S., Stevens, C., & The Off Pink Collective. (Eds.). (1996). *Bisexual horizons: Politics, histories, lives.* London: Lawrence & Wishart.

Office for National Statistics. (2019, January 21). Sexual orientation, UK: 2017: Experimental statistics on sexual orientation in the UK in 2017 by region, sex, age, marital status, ethnicity and socio-economic classification. Retrieved from www.ons.gov.uk/peoplepopulationandcommunity/culturalidentity/sexuality/bulletins/sexualidentityuk/2017

Okoli, O. H., Odumodu, N. C., Eze, J. E., & Emma-Echiegu, B. N. (2017). Role of sexual orientation on sexual-risk behaviour among at-risk young people in selected campus relaxation centres in Anambra state. *African Psychologist: An International Journal of Psychology and Allied Professions, 7*(1), 144–186.

Orndorff, K. (Ed.). (1999). *Bi lives: Bisexual women tell their stories.* Tucson: Sharp Press.

Pasquier, M. (2018, October 27). Explore the spectrum: Guide to finding your ace community. Retrieved from www.glaad.org/amp/ace-guide-finding-your-community

Persson, T. J., & Pfaus, J. G. (2015). Bisexuality and mental health: Future research directions. *Journal of Bisexuality, 15*(1), 82–98. doi:10.1080/15299716.2014.994694

Petford, B. (2003). Power in the darkness: Some thoughts on the marginalization of bisexuality in psychological literature. *Lesbian and Gay Psychology Review, 4*(2), 5–13.

Pieper, M., & Bauer, R. (2006). *Polyamory and mono-normativity: Results of an empirical study of non-monogamous patterns of intimacy.* Unpublished article.

Ritchie, A., & Barker, M. (2006). "There aren't words for what we do or how we feel so we have to make them up": Constructing polyamorous languages in a culture of compulsory monogamy. *Sexualities, 9*(5), 584–601. doi:10.1177/1363460706069987

Robinson, M. (2013). Polyamory and monogamy as strategic identities. *Journal of Bisexuality, 13*(1), 21–38. doi:10.1080/15299716.2013.755731

Ross, L. E., Dobinson, C., & Eady, A. (2010). Perceived determinants of mental health for bisexual people: A qualitative examination. *American Journal of Public Health, 100*(3), 496–502. doi:10.2105/AJPH.2008.156307

Rust, P. (1995). *Bisexuality and the challenge to lesbian politics: Sex, loyalty, and revolution.* New York: New York University Press.

Rust, P. C. (1992). The politics of sexual identity: Sexual attraction and behavior among lesbian and bisexual women. *Social Problems, 39*(4), 366–386. doi:10.2307/3097016

Rust, P. C. R. (Ed.). (2000). *Bisexuality in the United States: A social science reader.* New York: Columbia University Press.

Sage, A. (2019, August 10). French minister Marlène Schiappa mocked for saying brainy men turn her on. *The Times.* Retrieved from www.thetimes.co.uk/article/french-minister-marlene-schiappa-mocked-for-saying-brainy-men-turn-her-on-jzfw8n782

Sprott, R. A., & Benoit Hadcock, B. (2018). Bisexuality, pansexuality, queer identity, and kink identity. *Sexual and Relationship Therapy, 33*(1–2), 214–232. doi:10.1080/14681994.2017.1347616

Storr, M. (Ed.). (1999). *Bisexuality: A critical reader.* London: Routledge.

Swan, D. J. (2018a). Defining bisexuality: Challenges and importance of and toward a unifying definition. In D. J. Swan, & S. Habibi (Eds.), *Bisexuality: Theories, research, and recommendations for the invisible sexuality* (pp. 37–60). Cham: Springer. doi:10.1007/978-3-319-71535-3

Swan, D. J. (2018b). Models and measures of sexual orientation. In D. J. Swan, & S. Habibi (Eds.), *Bisexuality: Theories, research, and recommendations for the invisible sexuality* (pp. 19–36). Cham: Springer. doi:10.1007%2F978-3-319-71535-3_2

Swan, D. J., & Habibi, S. (Eds.). (2018). *Bisexuality: Theories, research, and recommendations for the invisible sexuality*. Cham: Springer. doi:10.1007/978-3-319-71535-3

Taylor, J. (2018). Out of the darkness and into the shadows: The evolution of contemporary bisexuality. *Canadian Journal of Human Sexuality*, *27*(2), 103–109. doi:10.3138/cjhs.2018-0014

Tucker, N., Highleyman, L., & Kaplan, R. (Eds.). (1995). *Bisexual politics: Theories, queries & visions*. Binghamton: Haworth Press.

Udis-Kessler, A. (1995). Identity/politics: A history of the bisexual movement. In N. Tucker, L. Highleyman, & R. Kaplan (Eds.), *Bisexual politics: Theories, queries & visions* (pp. 17–30). Binghamton: Haworth Press.

Weinberg, M. S., Williams, T. J., & Pryor, D. W. (1994). *Dual attraction: Understanding bisexuality*. New York: Oxford University Press.

Weise, E. R. (Ed.). (1992). *Closer to home: Bisexuality and feminism*. London: Airlift.

Wolff, C. (1977). *Bisexuality: A study*. London: Quartet Books.

Yoshino, K. (2000). The epistemic contract of bisexual erasure. *Stanford Law Review*, *52*(2), 353–461. doi:10.2307/1229482

2

A HISTORY OF BISEXUAL INVISIBILITY WITHIN SEXOLOGY AND PSYCHOLOGY

To understand current understandings of bisexuality it is necessary to explore how sexuality has been understood historically. The invisibility and erasure of bisexuality arguably have their roots in the work of the early sexologists. These men were the first to theorise sexuality and their contributions have been incredibly important and influential within sexology, psychology, and the wider social sciences. Their ideas formed the foundation of how sexualities and bisexuality were understood, and many of their theories are still apparent within contemporary conceptualisations of sexuality within wider Western culture. The key concept that dominated early first-wave sexologists' theories was that heterosexuality and homosexuality were opposites of each other. This binary categorisation of sexuality meant that sexologists, psychoanalysts, and psychologists alike seemed uncertain of what to do with bisexuality. This meant that bisexuality sometimes became pushed to the sidelines as they struggled to make it fit within their dichotomous model. Psychologists have continued to find it problematic to locate bisexuality (and pansexuality, asexuality, and plurisexualities) within this model because it does not allow for understandings beyond binaries. Interpretations of the early sexologists' theories in particular are not unequivocal, partly because their ideas were often complex, but also because those ideas often changed over the course of their lifetimes. Further, interpretations are often based on (translations of) their writings, including case studies of individuals, letters, pamphlets, and books. Nonetheless, these early sexologists' theories have created the foundations of bisexual invisibility. Although during second-wave sexology there began to be the potential for bisexuality to be understood in different ways, it nonetheless remained largely invisible within subsequent sex research.[1]

First-wave sexology

Before the work of the early sexologists the concepts which were understood were masculinity and femininity within the individual. Therefore, within early sexology, a bisexual person was understood to be someone with the characteristics of both masculinity and femininity (see Storr, 1999, 1999a, 1999b). Who someone was attracted to, or engaged in sexual behaviours with, was perceived as only an incidental factor which did not define their individual identities (Angelides, 2001; Oosterhuis, 2000; Terry, 1999). Therefore, in early discussions of bisexuality – or psychic hermaphroditism, as it was first termed – it was positioned as a third gender (Oosterhuis, 2000).

Third gender and gender inversion theories

Karl Heinrich Ulrichs (1825–1895; Box 2.1) was most noted for his theory of psychic hermaphroditism which was also known as the theory of the third sex, or uranism. The theory was based on German anatomists' ideas that during the early stages of development, human embryos are essentially hermaphrodites because their sexual organs are not differentiated (Brooks, 2012; Kennedy, 1981). Ulrichs suggested that during foetal development a division took place that resulted in men, women, and a "third sex" (Bullough, 1994).

BOX 2.1 KEY SEXOLOGISTS: KARL HEINRICH ULRICHS (1825–1895)

Karl Heinrich Ulrichs has been described as the first theorist of homosexuality, an early homosexual activist, and the forefather of the lesbian and gay liberation movement (Brooks, 2012; Sigusch, 2015). He was a German lawyer whose interest in sexology stemmed from his experiences of negative reactions to his own attraction to men. Consequently, his writings were largely in defence of homosexuality, and his aim was legal and social reform to decriminalise homosexual acts (Brooks, 2012; Oosterhuis, 2000). Ulrichs understood same-sex attraction as a naturally occurring phenomenon, and was a key figure in establishing formal sex and sexuality research (Brooks, 2012; Bullough, 1994; Sigusch, 2015). Ulrichs's work stemmed from theories of animal magnetism, physiology, mythology, and literature, as well as his personal beliefs, including that he had a female soul trapped within his own male body (Bullough, 1994; Sigusch, 2015). Ulrichs's third-gender theory was developed during the 1860s and was influential in how sexuality came to be conceptualised. It was also the first place in which the term psychic hermaphrodite was used to refer to attraction to men and women, rather than masculinity and femininity.

This third sex was portrayed as neither male nor female and included those who would come to be termed homosexuals (Angelides, 2001; Brooks, 2012). For Ulrichs, this third-sex theory provided an explanation of men who engaged in homosexual acts. Critically, Ulrichs theorised the third sex as "gender inverts" because of the "effect of a form of congenital degeneration whereby the *vita sexualis*, or procreative sex instinct, was thought to be inverted" (Angelides, 2001, p. 36). The notion of sexual instinct became a key idea in sexology, and was understood as a basic but powerful drive (Oosterhuis, 2012). The minds and bodies of the third gender were also portrayed as inverted. Therefore, a homosexual man was thought to be a female mind/soul trapped in a male body, and a homosexual woman a male mind/soul trapped in a female body (Fairyington, 2008; Weeks, 1989):

> [Ulrichs] accepted without question the idea that love directed towards a man must be a woman's love, and he saw it as a confirmation of his theory that he could detect "feminine" traits in himself and other homosexual males (for example, gestures, manner of walking, love of bright colours).
>
> *(Kennedy, 1981, p. 106)*

Taking terminology from Plato, Ulrichs created new terms with the aim of developing what he saw as positive language around same-sex desire (Brooks, 2012). Masculine heterosexual men were termed *Dioning*, and feminine heterosexual women *Dioningin*. He called (feminine) homosexual men *Urnings*, and (masculine) homosexual women *Urningin* (Brooks, 2012; Bullough, 1994; Kennedy, 1981). Initially, Ulrichs's third-gender theory only included feminine females and masculine males (heterosexuals) and feminine males and masculine females (homosexuals). Therefore, his ideas did not extend to anyone who did not fit within this dichotomy, and he originally had no explanation for what we now understand as bisexuality, pansexuality, and plurisexualities. However, through his contact with those who experienced same-sex desires, Ulrichs concluded that there needed to be more variation within his theory (Brooks, 2012). He developed an expansive nomenclature for people of the third sex to encapsulate more variety. This included masculine homosexual men (*Mannlings*) and feminine homosexual women (*Weiblings*) (Brooks, 2012). He also incorporated two types of "bisexual" men: conjunctive *Uranodionings* (who had tender and passionate feelings towards males and females), and disjunctive *Uranodionings* (who had tender feelings towards males, but whose passionate feelings were only towards females) (Brooks, 2012; Kennedy, 1981). This was based on the idea that there were "sex-drive germs in the embryo, one for tender love and one for passionate love, the direction of each being separated" (Kennedy, 1981, p. 107). However, in his attempt to incorporate all possibilities, his theory started to become overly complex (Kennedy, 1981).

Despite its limitations, Ulrichs's ideas of a third sex, and of hermaphroditism as the root of all sexualities, were widely distributed to professionals and elaborated upon by later researchers (Bullough, 1994; Kennedy, 1981; Oosterhuis, 2000). Particularly notably, Ulrichs's writings caught the attention of German-Austrian psychiatrist and sex researcher Richard von Krafft-Ebing (1840–1902; Box 2.2) (Brooks, 2012).

BOX 2.2 KEY SEXOLOGISTS: RICHARD VON KRAFFT-EBING (1840–1902)

Richard von Krafft-Ebing has been described as the founding father of sexology (Oosterhuis, 2012, 2015). He was a prominent German-Austrian psychiatrist who worked in mental asylums before establishing his own private practice and becoming a professor at various universities (Oosterhuis, 2015). His work was based on his many case studies of middle-/upper-class clients whose "perversions" and "deviant" behaviours he documented in his book *Psychopathia Sexualis* (1886/1997), intended for doctors and lawyers. Krafft-Ebing was an important influence in sexology, and played a key part in the medicalisation of homosexuality. This era saw a shift away from homosexual behaviours being theorised as morally deviant. Instead homosexuality became associated with physical or mental illness (Angelides, 2001; Weeks, 1989). Krafft-Ebing's work created a distinct division between the healthy heterosexual and the pathological homosexual. He has therefore been held responsible as "the founder of modern sexual pathology" (Angelides, 2001, p. 37; see also Oosterhuis, 2012). Krafft-Ebing has been credited with the shift both from the moral to the medical, and from sexual *behaviours* to personal sexual *identities* (Foucault, 1978; Oosterhuis, 2015; Weeks, 1989). He understood bisexuality as the origin of all sexualities (Oosterhuis, 2012).

Krafft-Ebing, influenced by Ulrichs, also considered homosexuality to be a matter of inverted masculinity and femininity (Angelides, 2001; Terry, 1999). On the basis of models of "normal" masculine males and feminine females, sexual inverts were understood to be masculine females and feminine males (Angelides, 2001). Krafft-Ebing believed that anything other than heterosexuality was indicative of a primitive state and regression to a lower life form (Terry, 1999). Drawing on biological and genetic theories, Krafft-Ebing agreed with Ulrichs that, during the early stages of development, all human embryos were hermaphrodites and that they became one sex or the other as they matured (Bullough, 1994; Hemmings, 2002; Oosterhuis, 2000, 2012). He became increasingly interested in the idea that psychic hermaphroditism was a part of the evolutionary process (Terry, 1999). He concluded that it was possible that humans' evolutionary ancestors had been hermaphrodite – or bisexual (Bullough, 1994; Oosterhuis, 2000, 2012). Consequently, he theorised bisexuality as the starting point from which all humans evolved (Bullough,

1994; Hemmings, 2002; Oosterhuis, 2000, 2012). This notion of bisexuality as the starting point of other sexualities may underpin notions of bisexuality as only a temporary state, as explored in Chapter 3.

Krafft-Ebing considered homosexuality to be degenerate and claimed that the cause was an underlying nervous disorder that included physical symptoms such as "dimensions, postures, gestures, and mannerisms that set them [homosexuals] apart from normal people" (Terry, 1999, p. 46; see also Kennedy, 1981). The lasting legacy of notions of homosexuality as a form of gender inversion – and of this inversion as visible on the physical body – is evident in cultural under-standings of sexuality (for example, images of butch lesbians and effeminate gay men; see Chapter 4). However, Krafft-Ebing was seemingly contrary about the physical aspects of the psychic hermaphrodite. It has sometimes been said that he believed that neither the psychological features nor the body of the psychic hermaphrodite would necessarily hint at any inversion (Oosterhuis, 2000). If this were the case, then his understanding was of homosexual bodies as marked by their inversion, in contrast to bisexual bodies as indistinguishable from any other and therefore invisible. However, some of Krafft-Ebing's case studies did discuss physical aspects of the psychic hermaphrodite – for example, that they might have "normal" genitals, but more masculine bodies than a "normal" heterosex-ual woman.

Krafft-Ebing's research comprised case studies of individuals who had been tried in court (Brennan & Hegarty, 2007). These case studies were published in *Psychopathia Sexualis* (Krafft-Ebing, 1886/1997). Here, psychic hermaphroditism was defined in terms of attraction – primarily same-sex desire, with some differ-ent-sex desire – rather than being described as part of the evolutionary process (Oosterhuis, 2000). The case studies listed under the heading of psychic herm-aphroditism demonstrate that he sometimes conceptualised bisexuality as a form of sexual attraction to men and women:

> Mrs M, forty-four years of age, claimed to be an instance illustrating that fact that in one and the same human being, be it man or woman, the inverted as well as the normal direction of sexual life may be combined. […] The first sentiments and emotions lay in the homosexual direction […] [but] her sexual inclinations turned now to woman, now to man.
>
> *(Krafft-Ebing, 1886/1997, pp. 171–174)*

Krafft-Ebing's ideas were hugely influential in the move away from an individ-ual's internal sexual inversion to their external sexual object choice. French phil-osopher Michel Foucault (1926–1984) has highlighted that this era of sexology represents a significant shift away from theorising sexual *behaviour* towards the notion of sexual *identity*:

Homosexuality appeared as one of the forms of sexuality when it was transposed from the practice of sodomy onto a kind of interior androgyny [...] The sodomite had been a temporary aberration; the homosexual was now a species.

(Foucault, 1978, p. 43)

This in turn created the notion of sexual identity as a fundamental aspect of the individual (Angelides, 2001; Brennan & Hegarty, 2009). It has been reported that, in later years, Krafft-Ebing became somewhat more lenient in his approach to homosexuality than in his earlier work. His writing reflected this when he began to position alternative sexual behaviours and identities as variations, rather than as pathological or deviant (Brennan & Hegarty, 2007, 2009; Oosterhuis, 2012). Iwan Bloch (1872–1922) more radically challenged the deviance models of this era when he moved away from medical and pathological viewpoints towards a tolerant outlook on sexuality. Bloch drew on a wide variety of historical and anthropological data and argued for a *Sexualwissenschaft*, or sexual science, based on historical, cultural, biological, and psychological data. His writings and ideas influenced subsequent sexologists, including Magnus Hirschfeld (1868–1935; Box 2.3) and Sigmund Freud (1856–1939; see below) (Bullough, 1994).

BOX 2.3 KEY SEXOLOGISTS: MAGNUS HIRSCHFELD (1868–1935)

German physician and sexologist Magnus Hirschfeld has been described as an influential but "often overlooked pioneer" in sexology (Bullough, 2003, p. 62). Influenced by Krafft-Ebing, his prolific writings made a significant contribution to sex research, although these were not translated into English until much later than those of other sexologists (Brennan & Hegarty, 2009; Bullough, 2003). One reason that he may have been overlooked was that Hirschfeld was homosexual and an advocate for tolerance. This may have contributed to his initially being understood by some as a political campaigner, rather than an expert scholar (Bullough, 2003). Perhaps due to this context, Hirschfeld sought to be scientific in his approach to social justice, and focused on biological explanations of homosexuality. In 1897 he co-founded the Scientific-Humanitarian Committee, with the aim of campaigning against the German law which criminalised sexual acts between men (Brennan & Hegarty, 2007, 2009). His published work included case studies and questionnaire research, on the basis of which he concluded that 4.5% of the population were bisexual (Brennan & Hegarty, 2007). He thought that all embryos were anatomically bisexual, but that through "normal" development most people became heterosexual (Brennan & Hegarty, 2007; Bullough, 2003).

Like Krafft-Ebing, Hirschfeld suggested that, in early embryotic development, all humans have characteristics of both sexes. He also believed that the characteristics of the "other" sex, and any potential for same-sex attraction, would recede during "normal" development and result in heterosexuality. He suggested that there were two exceptions to this. The first was homosexuality, where the desire for members of the same sex did not recede. The second was psychic hermaphroditism, where men and women could love and desire members of both sexes (Brennan & Hegarty, 2007; Bullough, 2003). The pioneering heterosexual British sex researcher and physician Henry Havelock Ellis (1859–1939; Box 2.4) was a contemporary of Hirschfeld. He was another sexologist noted for his tolerance of homosexuality, which he believed was an innate, natural, and harmless condition (Brickell, 2006; Bullough, 1994).

BOX 2.4 KEY SEXOLOGISTS: HENRY HAVELOCK ELLIS (1859–1939)

British doctor Henry Havelock Ellis's interest in sexology was partly inspired by his belief that sexual freedom held potential for happiness (Weeks, 2006). He was said to be tolerant of homosexuality and advocated social reform. His tolerance may partly have been related to his somewhat unconventional marriage to the lesbian lecturer and writer Edith Lees (Weeks, 2006; Wolff, 2009). He argued that sex and sexuality were natural and therefore beyond reproach. Ellis has been credited with a shift in how sexuality and sexual behaviour were understood within society (Weeks, 2006; Wolff, 2009). Like others before him, he believed that, during early development, males and females were indistinguishable (Tate, 2013). This mixture of male and female characteristics informed attraction: female characteristics underpinned attraction to men, and male characteristics attraction to women (Brickell, 2006). His ideas were based on a form of latent bisexuality as the common starting point for all humans (Storr, 1999a; Tate, 2013).

Ellis upheld gender inversion theories and used them to try to accommodate bisexuality (Storr, 1999a). Like others, Ellis primarily understood bisexuality as the root of heterosexuality and homosexuality. However, in later editions of his book *Studies in the Psychology of Sex* (Ellis, 1927), he wrote of bisexual individuals as a distinct category of people who are attracted to men and women:

> Those persons who are attracted to both sexes are now usually termed "bisexual", a more convenient term than "psycho-sexual hermaphrodite", which was formerly used. [...] There would thus seem to be a broad and simple grouping of all sexually functioning persons into three comprehensive divisions: the heterosexual, the bisexual, and the homosexual.
>
> *(Ellis, 1927, p. 2, p. 135)*

As a result of Ellis's categorisation, a system of describing different types of people as heterosexual, homosexual, and bisexual was becoming more established. This signified an important conceptual shift in how sexuality was conceptualised (Storr, 1999a). Nonetheless, in some of his writing it seems that Ellis proposed that some bisexual people could be considered fundamentally homosexual:

> There is sexual attraction to both sexes, a condition formerly called psycho-sexual hermaphroditism, but now more usually bisexuality. In such cases, *although there is pleasure and satisfaction in relationships with both sexes, there is usually a greater degree of satisfaction in connection with one sex. Most of the bisexual prefer their own sex.* It is curiously rare to find a person, whether man or woman, who by choice exercises relationships with both sexes and prefers the opposite sex. *This would seem to indicate that the bisexual may really be inverts.* In any case bisexuality merges imperceptibly into simple inversion.
>
> *(Ellis, 1927, p. 193, emphases added)*

In early sex research, the terms psychic hermaphrodite (and variations on the term) and bisexual were interlinked. The psychic hermaphrodite was often seen as the basis of all sexuality and as a temporary state. This notion is mirrored in contemporary cultural understandings that bisexual people will only temporarily identify as bisexual because they are really lesbians or gay men, as is discussed in Chapter 3. Both Krafft-Ebing's case studies and the subsequent work of Havelock Ellis show that by the early 20th century the term psychic hermaphrodite had been extended to have two meanings: (1) someone with the characteristics of both males and females; and (2) someone who experiences sexual attraction to both males and females. Eventually, the term psychic hermaphrodite began to disappear from use, and bisexuality became the dominant term (Storr, 1999a).

Universal human bisexuality

Sigmund Freud (Box 2.5) was a contemporary of Ellis and Hirschfeld. His work has been credited as the key factor in an important shift in sexual theory. This was because his explanations of homosexuality were firmly biological and congenital on one hand *and* psychological, social, and cultural on the other (Brickell, 2006; Moya & Larrain, 2016). Freud understood sexual instinct, or libido, as playing an important part in human activities and achievements (Brickell, 2006; Moya & Larrain, 2016). Some psychoanalysts were critical of Freud and interpreted his writing as suggesting that the sexual instinct was "the mother of all emotions", although others have suggested that this was not actually an idea endorsed by Freud himself (Lothane, 1997). Some critics who dismissed Freud's idea that all drives derive from sexual instinct branded psychoanalytic theory as pansexualism (Gay, 1995). It is important to emphasise here that pansexualism refers to the notion that all drives derive from sexual instinct and is therefore quite different from contemporary definitions of pansexuality as attraction to all genders or regardless of gender, as introduced in Chapter 1. As Freud's therapeutic model developed, his ideas became the dominant ones of the time. This may have been because the therapeutic application of his work allowed sexologists to make a living via the application of sexology, in the form of psychiatric treatment (Bullough, 1994).

BOX 2.5 KEY SEXOLOGISTS: SIGMUND FREUD (1856–1939)

Sigmund Freud was one of the most prominent sexologists, psychologists, and psychiatrists. His theories have been hugely influential within psychology and the wider culture (Smith & Hung, 2009). Freud was Austrian and studied medicine at the University of Vienna, where he would later become a professor (Pfäfflin, 2015). A neurologist and physiologist, he is best known for his personality theory (which included oral, anal, phallic, latency, and genital stages of psychosexual development) and for developing psychoanalytic theory (Smith & Hung, 2009). Sex and sexuality underpinned many of Freud's conceptual ideas, and he believed that sexual instinct was key to understanding both "normal" and "deviant" sexual behaviours. Freud was influenced by the work of early sexologists, including Krafft-Ebing, Hirschfeld, and Ellis. He notably rejected neurological, degenerative, and hereditary theories of pathology. Instead, he favoured psychological and psychobiological explanations of homosexuality as aspects of sexual development (Pfäfflin, 2015). Freud initially used the term hermaphroditism to refer to a combination of masculinity and femininity. However, like Ellis, Freud also talked about bisexuality as an identity, and believed that all humans naturally had a biological and psychological bisexual disposition (Young-Bruehl, 2001).

Similarly to others before him, Freud initially suggested that bisexuality was an innate and constitutional state at the root of all sexualities (Bullough, 1994). He believed that all children passed through a stage of homosexuality as part of their resolution of the Oedipus complex (Terry, 1999). Freud concluded that in "normal" human development there was a repression of same-sex desire which led to heterosexuality, whereas homosexuality and bisexuality arose as a result of "abnormal" development. Bisexuality was understood as a psychological failure to "orientate" in one direction or the other (Fairyington, 2008). It has been argued that the term orientation is problematic for bisexuality because it implies that sexuality is unidirectional. Therefore, the term suggests attraction to only one gender, which reiterates the heterosexual/homosexual binary and makes bisexuality "nonsensical" (Waites, 2005, 2009, p. 146). Further, the idea of bisexuality as "abnormal development" and as a "failure" to orientate effectively positions bisexuality as only temporary, which conceivably informs understandings of bisexuality as neither a valid identity nor a permanent one (Hemmings, 2002; Rust, 1995; see also Chapter 3). However, in his later work, Freud also recognised bisexuality as a distinct identity:

> It is well known that at all times there have been, as there still are, human beings who can take as their sexual objects persons of either sex and that the one orientation is no impediment to the other. We call these people bisexual and accept the fact of their existence without wondering much at it. But we have come to know that all human beings are bisexual in this sense and that their libido is distributed between objects of both sexes [...] the libidinal impulses can take both directions without producing a clash.
>
> *(Freud, 1937, p. 396)*

Nonetheless, Freud still suggested that it was more common for heterosexuality and homosexuality within the individual to create "irreconcilable conflict. A man's heterosexuality will not tolerate homosexuality, and vice versa" (Freud, 1937, p. 396). This too may underpin notions of bisexuality as a state of confusion (see Chapter 3).

Some authors have concluded that, even though he regarded bisexuality as central to human sexuality, for Freud it was also "the mysterious heart" of psychoanalysis, which he was never able to explain satisfactorily (Storr, 1999b, p. 21). Freud's work represents the beginning of psychoanalytical theorising of sexuality, and other psychoanalysts took up his idea of bisexuality as a stage of psychosexual development. Austrian psychoanalyst Wilhelm Stekel (1868–1940) was a follower of Freud. Accordingly, his ideas mirrored Freud's, and he too discussed bisexuality in terms of attraction to males and females. He asserted that everyone was "innately bisexual", but took this a step further than Freud did. He argued that, if humans were by origin bisexual, then homosexuality and heterosexuality were the "troubled psychosexual states" (Fairyington, 2008, p. 268). To him, attraction to only one sex relied on the repression of the natural starting point of dual attraction and was therefore neurotic and unnatural (Brickell, 2006; Storr, 1999b). However, this idea does not seem to have been widely incorporated by other theorists (Fairyington, 2008). Instead, during the psychoanalytic era, bisexual individuals were commonly understood to be cowardly homosexuals "trying to adjust to societal norms" (Bullough, 1994, p. 178). From this, a link can be made between psychoanalytical theory and the contemporary notion of the cowardly bisexual, who is really homosexual but does not wish to be stigmatised as such (Hemmings, 2002; see also Chapter 3).

Second-wave sexology

The two world wars impacted on sexology in a variety of ways and were effectively a considerable setback for European sex researchers in particular (Bullough, 2003). While the 1940s saw a surge of interest in sex research in the US, it remained the case that little was occurring in Europe. To study sex remained taboo within society, but there was an increasing awareness of the importance of understanding human sexuality and sexual behaviour (Bullough, 1994). The next generation of US sex research saw a significant change in how bisexuality was conceptualised. Alfred Kinsey (1894–1956; Box 2.6) focused on sexual behaviours. He and his colleagues conducted over 18,000 interviews, in which they asked participants about their sexual histories and sexual lives (Bullough, 1994; Ericksen & Steffen, 1999).

BOX 2.6 KEY SEXOLOGISTS: ALFRED KINSEY (1894–1956)

Alfred Kinsey has been described as one of the most influential researchers of the 20th century (Bullough, 1994). Kinsey was a zoologist at Indiana University and studied gall wasps. With a background in taxonomy, he was interested in collating and cataloguing "facts" about sexual behaviour, based on his belief that there was a shortage of information about what people did and with whom (Ericksen & Steffen, 1999). A popular story, perhaps propagated by Kinsey himself to maintain his credentials as a "valid scientist", reports that his interest in sex came through his teaching on a university course about marriage (Ericksen & Steffen, 1999, p. 57). However, he had an interest in sex research long before the course began (Ericksen & Steffen, 1999). He started asking students about their sexual histories, and this developed into his research with around 18,000 people (Bullough, 1994). Kinsey was a sexual libertarian who considered sex to be natural, and therefore all sexual behaviours to be normal (Ericksen & Steffen, 1999). He avoided theorising the origins or meanings of sexuality for fear of being open to abuse from medical and religious sources. However, it has been reported that he saw sexuality as the outcome of a combination of biological and cultural influences (Dodge, Reece, & Gebhard, 2008; Ericksen & Steffen, 1999). Perhaps surprisingly, Kinsey spoke only briefly about bisexuality per se, but he believed that all humans had the potential to be bisexual.

Sexuality as a continuum

The Kinsey reports on *Sexual Behavior in the Human Male* (Kinsey, Pomeroy, & Martin, 1948) and *Sexual Behavior in the Human Female* (Kinsey, Pomeroy, Martin, & Gebhard, 1953) offered significant potential for a move away from binary models towards a continuum theory of sexuality. A key finding from the interviews was that 37% of men had engaged in one or more physical sexual encounters with another man to the point of orgasm during their adult lives (Kinsey et al., 1948, p. 21). Approximately another 13% of the adult men reported that they had responded erotically to other men despite not having had sexual contact with them (Kinsey et al., 1948, p. 650). In the female data, 28% of women reported that they had experienced same-sex arousal (Kinsey et al.,

1953). These statistics surprised Kinsey and his colleagues, and shocked scientists and the public, because homosexual behaviours had been considered far rarer than these findings indicated. Kinsey was confident that these figures were robust (Kinsey et al., 1948). However, his sampling has been heavily criticised, and it may be that he overestimated how common same-sex sexual behaviour was (Ericksen & Steffen, 1999).

Kinsey was the first to offer ideas which really challenged the underpinning dichotomous models of sexuality, rather than trying to fit all sexualities within this binary conceptualisation (Rust, 1995). Kinsey highlighted that, if someone was known to have had even a single same-sex experience, then they tended to be considered homosexual (Kinsey et al., 1948, p. 647). His results showed that very few of the sample were exclusively homosexual or heterosexual. He suggested that this reliance on "two heads" (e.g., homosexual and heterosexual) overlooked the "endless gradations that actually exist" (Kinsey et al., 1948, p. 650). In *Sexual Behavior in the Human Female*, Kinsey wrote that there were a considerable number of people who had homosexual *and* heterosexual attractions or behaviours – sometimes sequentially and sometimes simultaneously (Kinsey et al., 1953). Kinsey has been credited with validating the range of potential for human sexuality, and for problematising binary understandings of sexuality:

> Many of those who are academically aware of it still fail to comprehend the realities of the situation. It is characteristic of the human mind that it tries to dichotomize in its classification of phenomena. Things are either so, or they are not so. Sexual behavior is either normal or abnormal, socially acceptable or unacceptable, heterosexual or homosexual; and many persons do not want to believe that there are gradations in these matters.
>
> *(Kinsey et al., 1953, p. 469)*

Kinsey argued that, rather than only two distinct categories of sexuality, there were wide variations:

> Males do not represent two discrete populations, heterosexual and homosexual. The world is not to be divided into sheep and goats. Not all things are black nor all things white. It is a fundamental of taxonomy that nature rarely deals with discrete categories. Only the human mind invents categories and tries to force facts into separated pigeon-holes. The living world is a continuum in each and every one of its aspects. The sooner we learn this concerning human sexual behavior the sooner we shall reach a sound understanding of the realities of sex.
>
> *(Kinsey et al., 1948, p. 639)*

His rejection of binary categorisations of sexuality led him to develop an alternative categorisation system, based on a continuum between heterosexual and homosexual (Kinsey et al., 1948). The renowned seven-point Kinsey scale (which can be seen on the website of the Kinsey Institute: https://kinseyinstitute.org/research/publications/kinsey-scale.php) ranges from exclusively heterosexual (Kinsey 0) to exclusively homosexual (Kinsey 6), with variations in between. The midpoint of 3 represented equal heterosexuality and homosexuality. He classed the remaining numbers as graduations of sexuality based on "overt sexual experience and/or […] psychosexual reactions" (Kinsey et al., 1948, p. 647). It has been noted that intermediary points between the specifications on the scale were also used (e.g., between 2 and 3, or 4 and 5). This was done both by participants when rating themselves, and by researchers who sometimes (re)assigned ratings to participants after their interviews (see Weinrich, 2014). He also saw an individual's position on the scale as open to change over time, which indicates his belief in sexual fluidity (Ericksen & Steffen, 1999).

Despite drawing attention to the limitations of dichotomous models of sexuality, the concept of bisexuality per se was still relatively invisible within Kinsey's work (Dodge et al., 2008). It has been noted that in *Sexual Behavior in the Human Male* (Kinsey et al., 1948), Kinsey "revealed major insights into bisexual behavior and orientation without ever using the word *bisexual*" (Dodge et al., 2008, p. 180). This was despite (or perhaps because of) claims that Kinsey was bisexual himself and therefore likely to have had a personal interest in bisexuality. He is also said to have disliked the term bisexual. This may have been partly because of his broader rejection of sexual identity labels, which he deemed unhelpful, because they could not capture the fluidity and diversity of sexual desire and behaviour (Dodge et al., 2008). While less widely written about, Kinsey also designated a "category x" to capture participants who were described in *Sexual Behavior in the Human Female* as sexually unresponsive to "either heterosexual or homosexual stimuli" (Kinsey et al., 1953, p. 407; see also Kinsey et al., 1948; Weinrich, 2014). This may represent the first acknowledgement of what would now be considered asexuality.

Kinsey's work has been hugely influential in its contribution to understandings of sexuality and instigated much discussion and future research (Bullough, 1994). However, as is evidenced in contemporary understandings of bisexuality, his continuum model did not immediately dislodge binary understandings of sexuality, and "the wall between gay and straight didn't exactly come tumbling down" (Fairyington, 2008, p. 267).

Early gay-affirmative research

During the 1950s and 1960s, what could be considered the first gay- and lesbian-affirmative research was conducted by pioneering psychologists Evelyn Hooker (1957) and June Hopkins (1969). In Hooker's (1957) research, expert clinicians were unable to distinguish between the projective test results of 30 matched pairs of heterosexual and homosexual men. These findings evidenced that gay men could not be deemed psychologically unhealthy. Hooker's results have been noted to be hugely important. Her findings played a part in the removal of homosexuality as a mental illness from the American Psychiatric Association's *Diagnostic and Statistical Manual* and changed how sexuality was understood by psychologists and others. The research findings were also used to argue more widely that homosexuality was not an illness. Similarly, the results of Hopkins's research with lesbian and heterosexual women showed that, on the basis of personality tests, neither lesbians nor heterosexual women were neurotic (Hopkins, 1969). Alongside psychological research came significant efforts by lesbian and gay liberation movements, which resulted in somewhat of a societal shift towards the recognition and validation of lesbian and gay identities (Floyd & Szymanski, 2007; Kimmel & Garnets, 2003). However, Hooker was keen to only include homosexual and heterosexual participants. Therefore, she eliminated heterosexual participants who had had more than one same-sex experience, and homosexual participants who had had more than three different-sex experiences. Hopkins (1969) utilised the Kinsey scale (see above) in her research. She categorised those between 0 and 2 as heterosexual, and those between 4 and 6 as homosexual. Those who rated themselves in the middle of the scale were eliminated from the study. While hugely significant, this early lesbian- and gay-affirmative research did not meaningfully include bisexuality.

Ignoring and minimising bisexuality: Laboratory research and sex surveys

Despite the potential that Kinsey's work provided for further theorising of sexuality, subsequent sexologists did not immediately choose to engage with theory, or to explore Kinsey's ideas around breaking down binaries and acknowledging variation and fluidity (Blumstein & Schwartz, 1976). There was a turn to alternative methods when William Masters (1915–2001) and Virginia Johnson (–1925–2013) (Box 2.7) conducted their laboratory research (Masters & Johnson, 1966/1981). They directly observed over 600 men and women engaging in masturbation and sexual intercourse. They measured physiological changes in the body, including heart rate, blood pressure, vaginal lubrication, and penile circumference, among others. They went on to develop a model of human response, which included four phases (excitement, plateau, orgasm, and resolution) (Both, 2015; Masters & Johnson, 1966/1981).

BOX 2.7 KEY SEXOLOGISTS: WILLIAM MASTERS (1915–2001) AND VIRGINIA JOHNSON (1925–2013)

The initial interests of US gynaecologist William Masters and researcher Virginia Johnson were primarily in how the human body responded physiologically during sexual arousal. They believed that this knowledge would allow people to overcome their sexual "problems" (Bullough, 1994). Their work is most notable for their development of a model of the "Human Sexual Response Cycle" (Masters & Johnson, 1966/1981). The key contribution of Masters and Johnson was a greater understanding of human physiology. They have also been credited with acknowledging sexual pleasure and making sex research and sex therapy acceptable. It has been argued that they led the way for future sexologists' work in education, research, and therapy (Both, 2015; Bullough, 1994).

However, their work has been heavily critiqued for privileging the biological and physiological, and for their pathologisation of homosexuality and their wider hetero/sexist assumptions (see Boyle, 1993; Tiefer, 2004). Masters and Johnson rarely mentioned bisexuality. Their 1979 book *Homosexuality in Perspective* included an index entry for bisexuality, but the reader was directed to the "ambisexual study group" (Masters & Johnson, 1979, p. 438). This small group of 12 participants was described as having no particular preference for partner gender. By using the term ambisexual, and defining it as a lack of preference, Masters and Johnson effectively rendered bisexuality invisible. However, they may have chosen this terminology following Blumstein and Schwartz (1976, 1977), who had advocated the term ambisexual to capture the idea that those who engaged in sexual behaviours with more than one sex/gender did not necessarily have an equal interest in men and women. Nevertheless, in their own writing Blumstein and Schwartz chose the "popular term *bisexual*" (Blumstein & Schwartz, 1976, p. 172, emphasis in original), which they reported had "already become entrenched in our language" (Blumstein & Schwartz, 1977, p. 32). Blumstein and Schwartz's choice to use the term bisexual may have contributed to some of the earliest recognition of bisexuality as a distinct identity within academic research, as discussed in Chapter 1.

Kinsey's use of survey methodology did prompt other sexuality researchers to choose similar methods for surveying sexual behaviour. However, the minimisation of bisexuality was also evident in these subsequent sex surveys (e.g., Hite, 1976; Janus & Janus, 1993). Perhaps the most notable of these was *The Hite Report* (Hite, 1976). Hite's work made an important contribution both to sexology and to wider cultural understandings of sexuality, and she became a household name. Hite conducted questionnaire research to explore women's sexualities and how women felt during sexual activities. Bisexual women were included, with 9% of respondents reported to have had sexual experiences with men and women, or to identify as bisexual. However, the inclusion of bisexuality was often minimal. The overall data from bisexual women was presented as a subsection of the content discussing lesbian women. Only two bisexual women were cited in more depth, and these excerpts were rather perfunctory, so did not contain enough information to provide meaningful accounts of their experiences (Hite, 1976).

From the mid-1970s there started to be a focus on bisexual people and research which validated bisexuality. As introduced in Chapter 1, a variety of publications by activists and academics started to evidence the existence, and explore the complexities, of bisexuality. However, despite an ever-increasing body of affirmative bisexual research, many researchers continue to amalgamate bisexual people's results with those of lesbian and gay people or heterosexual people. This overlooks the potential distinctiveness of bisexual people's experiences and renders bisexuality invisible (Barker et al., 2012). Even as bisexuality has become somewhat more visible within academic research and the wider culture, so too has it often been denigrated and dismissed, as discussed in the next chapter.

Note

1 This is not the first time that I have written about the work of first-wave and second-wave sexologists in relation to bisexuality. Helen Bowes-Catton and I previously published a chapter on this topic which includes similar content: Bowes-Catton, H., & Hayfield, N. (2015). Bisexuality. In C. Richards, & M. J. Barker (Eds.), *The Palgrave handbook of the psychology of sexuality and gender* (pp. 42–59). Basingstoke: Palgrave Macmillan.

References

Angelides, S. (2001). *A history of bisexuality*. Chicago: University of Chicago Press.

Barker, M., Yockney, J., Richards, C., Jones, R., Bowes-Catton, H., & Plowman, T. (2012). Guidelines for researching and writing about bisexuality. *Journal of Bisexuality*, *12*(3), 376–392.

Blumstein, P. W., & Schwartz, P. (1976). Bisexuality in women. *Archives of Sexual Behavior*, *5*(2), 171–181. doi:10.1007/BF01541873

Blumstein, P. W., & Schwartz, P. (1977). Bisexuality: Some social psychological issues. *Journal of Social Issues*, *33*(2), 30–45. doi:10.1111/j.1540-4560.1977.tb02004.x

Both, S. (2015). Masters and Johnson (the work). In P. Whelehan, & A. Bolin (Eds.), *The international encyclopedia of human sexuality* Hoboken: Wiley. doi:10.1002/9781118896877. wbiehs286

Boyle, M. (1993). Sexual dysfunction or heterosexual dysfunction? *Feminism and Psychology*, *3*(1), 73–88. doi:10.1177/0959353593031005

Brennan, T., & Hegarty, P. (2007). Who was Magnus Hirschfeld and why do we need to know? *History and Philosophy of Psychology*, *9*(1), 12–29.

Brennan, T., & Hegarty, P. (2009). Magnus Hirschfeld, his biographies and the possibilities and boundaries of "biography" as "doing history". *History of the Human Sciences*, *22*(5), 24–46. doi:10.1177/0952695109346642

Brickell, C. (2006). Sexology, the homo/hetero binary, and the complexities of male sexual history. *Sexualities*, *9*(4), 423–447. doi:10.1177/1363460706068043

Brooks, R. (2012). Transforming sexuality: The medical sources of Karl Heinrich Ulrichs (1825–95) and the origins of the theory of bisexuality. *Journal of the History of Medicine and Allied Sciences*, *67*(2), 177–216. doi:10.1093/jhmas/jrq064

Bullough, V. L. (1994). *Science in the bedroom: A history of sex research*. New York: Basic Books.

Bullough, V. L. (2003). Magnus Hirschfeld, an often overlooked pioneer. *Sexuality and Culture: An Interdisciplinary Journal*, *7*(1), 62–72. doi:10.1007/s12119-003-1008-4

Dodge, B., Reece, M., & Gebhard, P. H. (2008). Kinsey and beyond: Past, present, and future considerations for research on male bisexuality. *Journal of Bisexuality, 8*(3–4), 177–191. doi:10.1080/15299710802501462

Ellis, H. H. (1927). *Studies in the psychology of sex, volume II: Sexual inversion* (3rd ed.). Philadelphia: F. A. Davis.

Ericksen, J. A., & Steffen, S. A. (1999). *Kiss and tell: Surveying sex in the twentieth century*. London: Harvard University Press.

Fairyington, S. (2008). Kinsey, bisexuality, and the case against dualism. *Journal of Bisexuality, 8*(3–4), 267–272. doi:10.1080/15299710802501876

Floyd, J. Q., & Szymanski, L. A. (2007). Evelyn Gentry Hooker: The "hopelessly heterosexual" psychologist who normalized homosexuality. In E. A. Gavin, A. J. Clamar, & M. A. Siderits (Eds.), *Women of vision: Their psychology, circumstances, and success* (pp. 177–187). New York: Springer.

Foucault, M. (1978). *The history of sexuality: An introduction*. Harmondsworth: Penguin.

Freud, S. (1937). Analysis terminable and interminable. *International Journal of Psychoanalysis, 18*, 373–405.

Gay, P. (1995). On narcissism: An introduction. In P. Gay (Ed.), *The Freud reader* (pp. 545–562). London: Vintage.

Hemmings, C. (2002). *Bisexual spaces: A geography of sexuality and gender*. London: Routledge.

Hite, S. (1976). *The Hite report: A nationwide study on female sexuality*. New York: Macmillan.

Hooker, E. (1957). The adjustment of the male overt homosexual. *Journal of Projective Techniques, 21*(1), 18–31. doi:10.1080/08853126.1957.10380742

Hopkins, J. H. (1969). The lesbian personality. *British Journal of Psychiatry, 115*(529), 1433–1436. doi:10.1192/bjp.115.529.1433

Janus, S. S., & Janus, C. L. (1993). *The Janus report on sexual behavior*. Chichester: John Wiley and Sons.

Kennedy, H. C. (1981). The "third sex" theory of Karl Heinrich Ulrichs. *Journal of Homosexuality, 6*(1), 103–111. doi:10.1300/J082v06n01_10

Kimmel, D. C., & Garnets, L. D. (2003). What light it shed: The life of Evelyn Hooker. In L. D. Garnets, & D. C. Kimmel (Eds.), *Psychological perspectives on lesbian, gay and bisexual experiences* (pp. 31–49). New York: Columbia University Press.

Kinsey, A. C., Pomeroy, B. P., & Martin, C. E. (1948). *Sexual behavior in the human male*. Philadelphia: W. B. Saunders.

Kinsey, A. C., Pomeroy, B. P., Martin, C. E., & Gebhard, P. H. (1953). *Sexual behavior in the human female*. Philadelphia: W. B. Saunders.

Krafft-Ebing, R. (1886/1997). *Psychopathia sexualis: The case histories*. London: Velvet.

Lothane, Z. (1997). The schism between Freud and Jung over Schreber: Its implications for method and doctrine. *International Forum of Psychoanalysis, 6*(2), 103–115. doi:10.1080/08037069708405889

Masters, W. H., & Johnson, V. E. (1966/1981). *Human sexual response*. New York: Bantam Books.

Masters, W. H., & Johnson, V. E. (1979). *Homosexuality in perspective*. Boston: Little, Brown.

Moya, P., & Larrain, M. E. (2016). Sexuality and meaning in Freud and Merleau-Ponty. *International Journal of Psychoanalysis, 97*(3), 737–757. doi:10.1111/1745-8315.12494

Oosterhuis, H. (2000). *Stepchildren of nature: Krafft-Ebing, psychiatry, and the making of sexual identity*. London: University of Chicago Press.

Oosterhuis, H. (2012). Sexual modernity in the works of Richard von Krafft-Ebing and Albert Moll. *Medical History, 56*(2), 133–155. doi:10.1017/mdh.2011.30

Oosterhuis, H. (2015). Krafft-Ebing, Richard Freiherr von (1840–1902). In P. Whelehan, & A. Bolin (Eds.), *The international encyclopedia of human sexuality* Hoboken: Wiley. doi:10.1002/9781118896877.wbiehs254

Pfäfflin, F. (2015). Freud, Sigmund (1856–1939). In P. Whelehan, & A. Bolin (Eds.), *The international encyclopedia of human sexuality* Hoboken: Wiley. doi:10.1002/9781118896877.wbiehs163

Rust, P. C. (1995). *Bisexuality and the challenge to lesbian politics: Sex, loyalty, and revolution.* London: New York University Press.

Sigusch, V. (2015). Ulrichs, Karl Heinrich (1825–1895). In P. Whelehan, & A. Bolin (Eds.), *The international encyclopedia of human sexuality* Hoboken: Wiley. doi:10.1002/9781118896877.wbiehs523

Smith, C., & Hung, L. (2009). Freud, Sigmund (1856–1939). In J. O'Brien (Ed.), *Encyclopedia of gender and society* (pp. 334–335). Thousand Oaks: Sage.

Storr, M. (1999). Editor's introduction. In M. Storr (Ed.), *Bisexuality: A critical reader* (pp. 1–12). London: Routledge.

Storr, M. (1999a). Henry Havelock Ellis: Extracts from studies in the psychology of sex, volume I: Sexual inversion (1897) and from studies in the psychology of sex, volume II: Sexual inversion (1915). In M. Storr (Ed.), *Bisexuality: A critical reader* (pp. 15–19). London: Routledge.

Storr, M. (1999b). Sigmund Freud: Extract from three essays on the theory of sexuality: 1. The sexual aberrations (1905). In M. Storr (Ed.), *Bisexuality: A critical reader* (pp. 20–27). London: Routledge.

Tate, C. C. (2013). Another meaning of Darwinian feminism: Toward inclusive evolutionary accounts of sexual orientations. *Journal of Social, Evolutionary, and Cultural Psychology,* 7(4), 344. doi:10.1037/h0099184

Terry, J. (1999). *An American obsession: Science, medicine, and homosexuality in modern society.* London: University of Chicago Press. doi:10.7208/chicago/9780226793689.001.0001

Tiefer, L. (2004). Historical, scientific, clinical and feminist criticisms of "the human sexual response cycle" model. In M. S. Kimmel, & R. F. Plante (Eds.), *Sexualities* (pp. 52–64). Oxford: Oxford University Press.

Waites, M. (2005). The fixity of sexual identities in the public sphere: Biomedical knowledge, liberalism and the heterosexual/homosexual binary in late modernity. *Sexualities,* 8(5), 539–569. doi:10.1177/1363460705058393

Waites, M. (2009). Critique of "sexual orientation" and "gender identity" in human rights discourse: Global queer politics beyond the Yogyakarta Principles. *Contemporary Politics,* 15(1), 137–156. doi:10.1080/13569770802709604

Weeks, J. (1989). *Sex, politics and society: The regulation of sexuality since 1800* (2nd ed.). London: Longman.

Weeks, J. (2006, May 25). Ellis, (Henry) Havelock. *Oxford Dictionary of National Biography.* Retrieved from www.oxforddnb.com/view/10.1093/ref:odnb/9780198614128.001.0001/odnb-9780198614128-e-33009/version/1.

Weinrich, J. D. (2014). Notes on the Kinsey scale. *Journal of Bisexuality,* 14(3–4), 333–340. doi:10.1080/15299716.2014.951139

Wolff, K. B. (2009). Ellis, Havelock (1859–1939). In J. O'Brien (Ed.), *Encyclopedia of gender and society* (pp. 250–251). Thousand Oaks: Sage.

Young-Bruehl, E. (2001). Are human beings by nature bisexual? *Studies in Gender and Sexuality,* 2(3), 179–213. doi:10.1080/15240650209349175

3

INVISIBLE OR INVALIDATED

The marginalisation of bisexual identities

When bisexuality has become visible, it has often been within a framework of common cultural understandings which serve to discredit it. This has sometimes been to the extent of dismissing bisexuality entirely, which therefore makes it invisible once again (Alarie & Gaudet, 2013; Klesse, 2011). Academics and activists have repeatedly drawn attention to the marginalisation and oppression of bisexual people, and some have noted that the roots of this lie within binary and dichotomous models of sexuality, as introduced in Chapter 1. In this chapter the focus is on the ways in which bisexuality has often been made invisible and/or invalidated within the wider culture and the implications of this for bisexual people.

The concept of homophobia developed during the late 1960s and early 1970s to refer to fear of homosexuality and prejudice against homosexual people (MacDonald, 1976; Smith, 1971; Weinberg, 1972; see also Herek, 2004). This body of research has tended to be focused mainly on gay men. The notion of lesophobia – to specifically refer to fear of lesbian sexuality and prejudice against lesbian women – has largely been overlooked (Kasl, 2002). It was not until the 1990s that the term biphobia was coined to capture prejudice specifically against bisexual people (Bennett, 1992; Eliason, 1997; Ochs, 1996; Box 3.1). To date, the terms panphobia and aphobia have seemingly yet to be referred to in academic sources. Nonetheless, researchers have started to identify prejudice in relation to pansexual and asexual people. These prejudices may be both similar to and different from the ways in which bisexual people are marginalised (e.g., Belous & Bauman, 2017; Gonel, 2013; Gupta, 2017; Lapointe, 2017).

BOX 3.1 KEY TERMS: BIPHOBIA, BINEGATIVITY, AND BISEXUAL MARGINALISATION

The term biphobia is believed to have been first used by Kathleen Bennett to refer to "the denigration of bisexuality" as a valid identity (Bennett, 1992, p. 207). Its definition has developed to refer to prejudice against, dislike of, or negative attitudes towards bisexuality and bisexual people (Bennett, 1992; Eliason, 1997; Mulick & Wright, 2002). Biphobia is the most recognised term among mainstream quantitative psychology researchers, and outside academia, because it mirrors the terms homophobia and transphobia. Indeed, in recent years recognition of biphobia has been included in some equality campaigns and social policy documents (see Barker, 2015).

Binegativity and bisexual marginalisation are alternative terms which more broadly refer to the marginalisation and stigmatisation of bisexuality (Klesse, 2011; Lytle, Dyar, Levy, & London, 2017; Molina et al., 2015; Yost & Thomas, 2012). Binegativity was seemingly first used by Susan Morrow, a US counselling psychologist and qualitative researcher (Morrow, 2000). She argued that the term phobia was based on the notion of (irrational) fear, and that this was restrictive because it oversimplified the complexities and underpinnings of negativity. She also drew on Celia Kitzinger's (1987) argument that the concept of a phobia is implicitly positioned as a psychological or personality disorder, located within an individual person. The notion that "attitudes" and phobias towards particular groups are individual phenomena overlooks interactional processes and the social, cultural, and political factors which underpin oppression (see also Kitzinger & Perkins, 1993; Speer & Potter, 2000). These types of critique have informed critical/qualitative social psychologists, sociologists, and others, who have drawn on terminology such as binegativity and bisexual marginalisation over biphobia to better capture their recognition of the nuances and complexities of bisexual oppression (Eliason, 2000; Hayfield, Clarke, & Halliwell, 2014; Klesse, 2011; Yost & Thomas, 2012). However, more recent biphobia research sometimes moves beyond oversimplified definitions by expanding beyond the individual to include societal considerations and explanations (Klesse, 2011).

A sizeable body of literature on homophobia (as noted above, mostly in relation to gay men) has been published since the late 1970s (e.g., Channing & Ward, 2017; Formby, 2013; Herek, 1984, 1998, 2004, 2015; Rosenberg, Gates, Richmond, & Sinno, 2017; Shabazz, 1979; Tully & Albro, 1979; Warwick & Aggleton, 2014). While a large proportion of the existing bisexuality literature is focused on biphobia, it is nonetheless only a small body of psychological research compared with that on homophobia. Table 3.1 shows the number of academic papers identified by searching the academic database PsycINFO for the terms homophobia and biphobia. This demonstrates that biphobia has received relatively little attention within academic research and is therefore relatively invisible compared with

TABLE 3.1 Results of academic searches for homophobia and biphobia using PsycINFO academic database

Decade	Homophobia in title	Homophobia in title or abstract or keywords	Biphobia in title	Biphobia in title or abstract or keywords
1971–1980	10	17	0	0
1981–1990	62	207	0	0
1991–2000	178	616	3	6
2001–2010	299	1,078	31	31
2010–2018	268	1,250	12	69
Totals	**817**	**3,168**	**46**	**106**

homophobia. Prejudice and discrimination are important areas of study. As increasing numbers of people identify with bisexuality, pansexuality, asexuality, and other plurisexual identities, researchers must be inclusive of these identities, as well as continuing to focus on lesbian and gay people.

What do we know about biphobia, bisexual negativity, and bisexual marginalisation?

Much of the earliest writing on biphobia tended to be anecdotal personal reflections, or theoretical discussion (Eliason, 1997; Eliason & Elia, 2011). When researchers began empirical investigations of biphobia, studies were mainly quantitative in design and drew on Likert scales to investigate non-bisexual people's attitudes towards bisexuality and bisexual people (Boxes 3.2 and 3.3). More recently, the focus has moved to bisexual people's own experiences of marginalisation. This body of empirical research has mainly been conducted in the US, with some studies conducted in the UK, but fewer studies elsewhere in the world. This means that much of what we know relates specifically to a (mainly White and) Western cultural context. In recent years, studies have continued to be predominantly quantitative, with some qualitative research.

> **BOX 3.2 KEY PSYCHOLOGY STUDY: *THE PREVALENCE AND NATURE OF BIPHOBIA IN HETEROSEXUAL UNDER-GRADUATE STUDENTS* (ELIASON, 1997)**
>
> One of the first empirical studies on biphobia was conducted by US health psychologist Mickey Eliason. Two hundred and twenty-nine heterosexual undergraduate students (mainly women) completed Likert scale questionnaires about their attitudes towards lesbian, gay, and bisexual people. The key findings were:
>
> • Participants reported that they did not (knowingly) have any bisexual friends (76%) or acquaintances (64%).

- Accordingly, participants had little or no knowledge about bisexuality – which may explain why they frequently responded "I don't know" when asked to agree or disagree with statements about bisexual people.
- Biphobia and homophobia were correlated, but negative beliefs about bisexual people (especially men) were more prevalent than negative attitudes about lesbians and gay men.
- Half of the participants "rated bisexual women as acceptable", while the other half "rated them as unacceptable" (Eliason, 1997, p. 324).
- Overall, 61% of participants rated bisexual men as unacceptable. Heterosexual men were more likely than heterosexual women to rate bisexual men as unacceptable.
- Three-quarters of participants indicated that it was "unlikely" or "very unlikely" that they would have "a sexual relationship with a bisexual person they were really attracted to" (Eliason, 1997, p. 320).
- A majority of participants endorsed stereotypical statements about bisexual people, including that they were really gay or lesbian but afraid to admit it.

Eliason (1997) highlighted that the lack of accurate information about sexuality might be one explanation for relatively high levels of biphobia. Since publication, this early study has been cited over 300 times by other researchers.

BOX 3.3 MEASURING ATTITUDES TOWARDS BISEXUALITY AND BISEXUAL PEOPLE

Researchers (mainly in the US) have developed a number of attitude scales to investigate and evidence the existence of biphobia, and to measure its prevalence among lesbian, gay, heterosexual, and sometimes bisexual people.

Attitudes regarding bisexuality scale (Mohr & Rochlen, 1999)

US counselling psychologists Jonathan Mohr and Aaron Rochlen (1999) developed a scale to measure attitudes towards bisexuality by conducting a series of studies with students. The final scale includes 12 statements based on two factors. The first factor relates to the perceived *instability* of bisexuality as an identity. This includes statements such as "most (women/men) who identify as bisexual have not yet discovered their true sexual orientation" and "just like homosexuality and heterosexuality, bisexuality is a stable sexual orientation for (women/men)" (reversed) (p. 358). The second factor relates to *intolerance* of bisexuality, such as "bisexual (women/men) are sick" and "as far as I'm concerned bisexuality is *not* a perversion" (reversed) (p. 358). Participants were asked to agree or disagree with these statements on a five-point Likert scale, and their responses were statistically analysed. Mohr and Rochlen's key findings were that lesbian, gay, and heterosexual participants often agreed with statements to the effect that bisexuality was not a genuine identity and that bisexual people were incapable of monogamy. Since the scale was developed, other researchers have continued to utilise it (e.g., Lytle et al., 2017; Matsuda, Rouse, & Miller-Perrin, 2014), including to revise it for use within specific cultural contexts (e.g., Arndt & De Bruin, 2011).

Biphobia scale (Mulick & Wright, 2002)

A few years later, US psychologists Patrick Mulick and Lester Wright (2007) aimed to demonstrate that biphobia existed, to show that it was present in heterosexual and lesbian and gay communities, and to develop a scale to measure it. In order to trial and test the scale, a number of studies were conducted with convenience samples of bisexual, lesbian, gay, and heterosexual university students (most of whom were women). The final scale included 30 items for participants to agree or disagree with. These included "I do not like bisexual individuals", "you cannot trust a person who is bisexual", and "bisexual individuals are not capable of monogamous relationships" (p. 57). Mulick and Wright concluded that biphobia did exist in both heterosexual and lesbian and gay communities, and that this could result in difficult environments for bisexual people (Mulick & Wright, 2002, 2011). Researchers have since utilised the scale to explore a range of topics (e.g., Armstrong & Reissing, 2014; Yost & Thomas, 2012).

Common cultural understandings of bisexuality

These common cultural understandings of bisexuality have been developed from themes in the existing literature based on reports by activists and academics. However, to exemplify bisexual people's experiences of them, I use selected quotations from bisexual women who took part in my, Victoria Clarke, and Emma Halliwell's study on bisexual marginalisation (for details of the sample, see Chapter 1; for the full results, see Hayfield et al., 2014).

Bisexuality is an attention-seeking strategy for women to attract men

Bisexuality has sometimes been understood as purely a performance by sexually adventurous women to seek the attention of heterosexual men by kissing other women (Alarie & Gaudet, 2013; Wandrey, Mosack, & Moore, 2015; Wilkinson, 1996). Same-sex kissing between women is understood as flirtatious, fun, and frivolous, and reflects a flexible and fashionable version of (hetero)sexuality, sometimes referred to as heteroflexibility (Diamond, 2005; Farhall, 2018; Wilkinson, 1996). However, in the bisexual marginalisation study, Marie disassociated her own "true sexuality" from this version of bisexuality:

> I think there's a certain type of bisexuality that is visible and I don't think that's real bisexuality [...] so many of my female friends do this, they'll just get off with each other in front of guys to make guys like them [...] There's so much of a focus on, a sort of faux bisexuality as being something to attract men. The actual true sexuality is lost in that.
>
> *(Marie)*

This cultural understanding of bisexuality as a performative act of same-sex kissing has commonly been portrayed in mainstream mass media (Fahs, 2009; Farhall, 2018), with perhaps the most recognised examples being Britney Spears and Madonna kissing at the 2003 MTV Video Music Awards, and the lyrics of the 2008 Katy Perry version of the hit single "I kissed a girl" (Fahs, 2009; Rupp & Taylor, 2010). Other participants in our study also reported that these portrayals were misrepresentative of their lived experiences of bisexuality:

> I think we should be more visible, I think we should talk about it more, and *claim* it and say "no, no, no, *that* bisexual is not what I am" [...] and I *fuck*ing hate it, all that Katy Perry "I kissed a girl and I liked it, I hope my boyfriend doesn't mind it" and all this, it's like, "fuck off!"
>
> *(Lucy)*

The performance of bisexuality has been critiqued by scholars as an exploitation of women's sexuality in the interests of the male gaze and men's sexual fantasies (Fahs, 2009; Wilkinson, 1996). This understanding of bisexuality as attention seeking is often referred to in terms which locate bisexual identities as temporary, trendy, and experimental – such as bisexuality à la mode, barsexual, and bicurious (Diamond, 2005; Farhall, 2018; Rupp & Taylor, 2010; Wandrey et al., 2015; Wilkinson, 1996). Further, young women may come under pressure to "perform" bisexuality to titillate heterosexual men's fantasies. The term compulsory bisexuality was coined by Breanne Fahs (2009) to capture this phenomenon, which may even become a rite of passage (see also Alarie & Gaudet, 2013). This version of bisexuality dismisses the possibility of bisexuality as an ongoing or genuine identity.

Bisexuality is a temporary developmental phase and bisexual people are unable to commit to an identity

One of the most persistent misconceptions is that bisexuality does not exist as on ongoing identity, but instead is a temporary position on the path to being straight, or lesbian or gay (Anderson, McCormack, & Ripley, 2016; Eliason, 1997; McLean, 2008b; Rust, 1995). Those who "claim" to be bisexual – and more recently as pansexual too – are understood to be in a passing developmental phase. They are therefore perceived to be too immature to have realised their "true" identity or to have "made up their minds" about their sexuality (Hayfield et al., 2014; Lapointe, 2017; McLean, 2008b). Bisexual people are seen as failing to commit to heterosexuality or homosexuality, and it has been reported that both bisexual and pansexual people come under pressure to "choose a side" (Brown & Lilton, 2019; McLean, 2008b; Niki, 2018). This pressure is not welcomed:

> This woman [at a community event] just did this, like, really standard response, and she just totally laid into me, and said "you should just make your mind up, and so on, and so on, and so on" and I just said "well thanks for your understanding love".
>
> *(Lucy)*

It is perhaps more common for bisexual women to be understood as on a developmental path to a heterosexual identity and for bisexual men to be seen as in transition towards a gay identity (Alarie & Gaudet, 2013; Yost & Thomas, 2012). The notion of bisexuality as a temporary and inauthentic state is reflected in a number of expressions such as bi now, gay later (Brewster & Moradi, 2010; Niki, 2018) and gay, straight, or lying (Fahs, 2009; Niki, 2018; Spalding & Peplau, 1997). Other derogatory terms which position bisexuality as temporary include half-baked lesbian (Niki, 2018), and bisexual until graduation – a reference to women who (are perceived to) identify as bisexual only during university (e.g., Fahs, 2009; Wandrey et al., 2015). In all these iterations, bisexual identity is understood as a temporary pathway towards developmental maturity, when bisexuality will disappear and therefore become invisible once more.

Bisexual people are confused, cowardly, and unable to commit to LG(BTQ+) communities

A number of additional misconceptions about bisexuality also arise from the notion that bisexual people are in a temporary stage. Due to their perceived "failure" to orientate towards only one sex/gender, bisexual people are understood to be confused, emotionally immature, indecisive, or psychologically disturbed, as they allegedly flounder between straight and gay (Klesse, 2011; McLean, 2008a, 2008b; Rust, 1995; Zivony & Saguy, 2018). These understandings have even led to accusations that bisexual people are delusional in their belief that they are bisexual, or in denial of their "true" sexuality (Armstrong & Reissing, 2014; McLean, 2008b, p. 159). Participants in our study reported their experiences of encountering such understandings:

> You're just confused, it's a phase you're going through, it's not fair to the gay world, being a traitor. Why should we be negated? [...] And it suggests as well that there's something not quite right about us. That actually

we don't exist in our own right. Y'know that we are passing through, we will eventually realise that actually we're straight, or actually we're gay. Y'know, whereas actually, no, we're not. We're not.

(Blue)

Bisexual people may also face accusations from lesbian and gay people that they are too cowardly to commit or to "come all the way out" (Bradford, 2006, p. 19). Bisexual people's "claim" to be bisexual is interpreted as a strategy to avoid the social stigma often associated with being out and open as a lesbian or gay person (Bradford, 2006; Hayfield et al., 2014; Klesse, 2011; Niki, 2018). Therefore, bisexual people are understood as hiding behind heterosexual privilege, and as traitors who are failing to fully commit to their true identities, or to offer their solidarity to lesbian and gay communities (Bradford, 2006; Brewster & Moradi, 2010; McLean, 2007, 2008a; Niki, 2018; Ochs, 1996; Rust, 1995). They are accused of wanting the advantages of LGBTQ+ shared spaces alongside acceptance within the wider culture (Hemmings, 2002; Ochs, 1996). This also translates into understandings that bisexual people want "the best of both worlds" without fully committing to either (Hayfield et al., 2014; Israel & Mohr, 2004, p. 123; Rust, 1995).

Bisexual people are sex-obsessed, promiscuous, and unable to commit to monogamous relationships

Notions of bisexual people being unable to commit extend to bisexual people's commitment to their partners and their relationships. A common assumption is that because bisexual people are attracted to more than one sex/gender, they must therefore engage in (simultaneous) sexual activities with numerous people, of multiple genders, at all times. This sometimes becomes understood as almost a requirement for bisexual people to maintain (or prove) their bisexual identity (Eliason, 1997; Hayfield, Campbell, & Reed, 2018; Israel & Mohr, 2004; McLean, 2008b). These ideas underpin beliefs that bisexual people are sex-obsessed, hypersexual, promiscuous, and incapable of committing to monogamous relationships (Armstrong & Reissing, 2014; Hayfield et al., 2018; Israel & Mohr, 2004; Klesse, 2011; McLean, 2008b; Rust, 1995; Zivony & Saguy, 2018). What becomes inferred is that bisexual people cannot be content with one partner, are untrustworthy, and will inevitably cheat on their partners (Hayfield et al., 2018; Klesse, 2011; McLean, 2008a, 2008b; Rust, 1995; Spalding & Peplau, 1997). Some Internet sources define pansexuality as attraction to all genders, and then emphasise that someone who is pansexual will not necessarily be promiscuous (Belous & Bauman, 2017), perhaps in anticipation and defence of such an accusation. Bisexual people have sometimes worked to resist these conceptualisations (Eisner, 2013), and this was evident among some participants in our study:

If you're straight you fancy men, and if you're going out with a man no one kind of [says], "oh but you're just gonna go and sleep with loads of other men". In the same way, if you're gay, people aren't like "oh well you must actually just be using them and soon you're gonna drop them and sleep with someone else". Because that's not how heterosexual or lesbian and gay relationships are seen. Whereas the stereotype is that [as a bisexual person] you can't commit, or you don't want to commit, you just wanna go off with anyone, which I think's a real shame. Because it's not true (*laughs*).

(Marie)

What follows from the idea that bisexual people are sex-obsessed and promiscuous is that they must be sexually adventurous and kinky (McLean, 2008b; Spalding & Peplau, 1997). Therefore, bisexual people are understood to privilege sexual activities and casual sexual relationships over emotions and emotional relationships. Further, there has been a history of bisexual people (in particular bisexual men) being understood as spreaders of disease (Dodge et al., 2016; Israel & Mohr, 2004; Ochs, 1996; Watson, Allen, Pollitt, & Eaton, 2019). Those who are bisexual may find that these assumptions are made about them both when they *are* non-monogamous and when they are simply *assumed* to be non-monogamous. These interrelated ideas around sex and promiscuity further demonise and discredit bisexual people.

Bisexual people are greedy

Another common cultural understanding is that bisexual people are greedy. There are two versions of this misconception. In the first, assumptions about promiscuity are taken to mean that bisexual people want lots of sex and are therefore greedy (Alarie & Gaudet, 2013; Barker, 2015; Klesse, 2011; Rust, 1995). In this version, the greedy bisexual is accused of having an insatiable sexual appetite, and understood as unscrupulously interested in sexual activities with "anything that moves" (Anderson et al., 2016; Eliason, 2000; Friedman et al., 2017; Israel & Mohr, 2004; McLean, 2008a). In turn, they may be "seen as romantically fickle" (Spalding & Peplau, 1997, p. 612) and accused of "having their cake and eating it too", on the assumption that they engage in sexual activities with more than one sex/gender and with more than one person at any one time (Comeau, 2012; Spalding & Peplau, 1997). Some bisexual people will be in monogamous relationships whereas others will be in consensually non-monogamous/polyamorous relationships (Barker & Langdridge, 2010; Hayfield et al., 2018; McLean, 2007; Ritchie & Barker, 2006). Cultural representations often link consensual non-monogamies and polyamories with dishonesty, infidelity, or even neuroticism and pathology (Ritchie & Barker, 2006). Relationship models which involve multiple partners are often understood negatively within Western culture (e.g., Grunt-Mejer & Campbell, 2016), as referred to by some of our participants:

It's kind of sex negativity and greed, because I think bisexuality's seen as this hypersexual identity. And so if people are bisexual, and if they're talking about it, then it must mean that they're not monogamous, and therefore it must mean that they're promiscuous, and that's all terrible because we *mustn't* ever have sex apart from the one person, blah blah blah, or at least if we do it, we mustn't admit to it, and we must feel very terrible about it.

(Claire)

The second way in which bisexual people are positioned as greedy is through the pleasures that arise from same-sex encounters and from being members of LGBTQ+ communities (i.e., without the stigma associated with being "out" as gay or lesbian). This also links back to the idea that bisexual people are cowardly because they are "copping out of being out" and failing to affiliate with lesbian and/or gay communities (Hemmings, 2002; Rust, 1995).

In sum, it has been identified that bisexual people are perceived in a number of negative ways. When bisexuality becomes visible, it is seemingly either dismissed or discredited, and hence becomes erased and invisible or invalidated. These discreditations and dismissals are based on a range of interrelated negative attributions (e.g., as immature, confused, undecided, cowardly, deluded, emotionally or mentally unstable), or on notions of bisexuality as a hedonistic identity (e.g., as attention-seeking, greedy, promiscuous, sex-obsessed, incapable of love or commitment, and spreading disease). These capture some of the most dominant negative understandings of bisexuality commonly identified by activists and academics and reported on in the psychological literature.

The nuances of biphobia, bisexual negativity, and bisexual marginalisation

Biphobia, bisexual negativity, and bisexual marginalisation are nuanced according to a range of factors. Researchers have frequently reported that bisexual people experience double discrimination (Box 3.4), but recent research indicates that heterosexual people are sometimes more negative about bisexuality than lesbian and gay people (Dodge et al., 2016; Friedman et al., 2014; Hertlein, Hartwell, & Munns, 2016; Roberts, Horne, & Hoyt, 2015). One study included asexual participants and found that they too may hold negative stereotypes about bisexuality, although less so than lesbian and gay people (De Bruin & Arndt, 2010). It is important to remember that those with asexual spectrum identities may themselves identify as bisexual, biromantic, pansexual, or panromantic (Carrigan, 2015), and may face prejudices which are both similar to and different from allosexual bisexual people. Perhaps unsurprisingly, bisexual people have been reported to have the least negative attitudes towards bisexuality (Friedman et al., 2014). Nonetheless, binegativity (see Box 3.1) may also be internalised by bisexual people whereby they are understood to (perhaps unknowingly) internalise negative societal beliefs about bisexuality and apply them to both themselves and other bisexual people. Research has identified that internalised binegativity may be linked to depression, low self-esteem, and psychological distress (see Baumgartner, 2017; Brewster, Moradi, DeBlaere, & Velez, 2013; Lambe, Cerezo, & O'Shaughnessy, 2017).

BOX 3.4 KEY TERMS: DOUBLE DISCRIMINATION AND MULTIPLE DISCRIMINATION

The term double discrimination refers to the idea that bisexual people can experience discrimination *both* from people in lesbian and gay communities *and* from people in the wider heterosexual culture. The term was seemingly first used by US academic and activist Robyn Ochs (1996) in her essay "Biphobia: It goes more than two ways". She argued that bisexuality threatens the social order by challenging binary understandings of sexuality as either straight or gay and that it is this which underpins many negative understandings of bisexuality. Ochs's (1996) discussion of double discrimination has been widely taken up. When Mulick and Wright (2002) developed the biphobia scale (see Box 3.3), they concluded not only that discrimination existed in both heterosexual and lesbian and gay communities, but also that bisexual people may experience biphobia from lesbian and gay people, as well as homophobia *and* biphobia from the wider heterosexual culture (Mulick & Wright, 2011). Bisexual people are therefore likely to have distinctive experiences of prejudice (Friedman et al., 2014; Hayfield et al., 2014; Mulick & Wright, 2002, 2011; Rust, 1995). Bisexual people have reported that, as a consequence of double discrimination, they feel rejected from both LG(BTQ) communities and heterosexual culture (Hayfield et al., 2014; McLean, 2008a).

Bisexual people may also experience what I would consider to be *multiple* discrimination according to intersections of gender, race and ethnicity, disability, class, and other factors. To date, there is a paucity of research in these areas (e.g., Doan Van, Mereish, Woulfe, & Katz-Wise, 2019; Ross, Dobinson, & Eady, 2010). In one study with participants attracted to more than one gender (e.g., bisexual, pansexual, or queer), trans and cisgender women reported more discriminatory incidents of sexual harassment, physical threat, and sexual violence than cisgender men. Only 19% of "trans/non-binary/other" participants reported that they had experienced "no discrimination," compared to 31% of cisgender women and 50% of cisgender men. Trans participants also had the highest incidence of sexual harassment, physical threat, sexual violence, and physical assault, compared with any other group in the study (Doan Van et al., 2019, p. 165). In other research, people of Colour reported more discrimination in healthcare than White participants; the authors also noted that discrimination related to more than one aspect of their identities (e.g., sexuality, gender, ethnicity). Given the lack of acceptance or belonging that bisexual people report feeling, it is perhaps unsurprising that these forms of discrimination have been linked to mental health issues within bisexual populations (Barker, Bowes-Catton, Iantaffi, Cassidy, & Brewer, 2008; Doan Van et al., 2019; Friedman et al., 2014; Morrison, Gruenhage, & Pedersen, 2016; Mulick & Wright, 2011).

There are also differences in how bisexual people are perceived according to their own sex/gender and the sex/gender of the perceiver. Bisexual men may be perceived as in a transitional phase and "really gay", whereas bisexual women may be understood as performing bisexuality and "really heterosexual" – particularly by lesbian women (Alarie & Gaudet, 2013; Yost & Thomas, 2012). Bisexual men have been seen as less socially acceptable than bisexual women (Alarie & Gaudet, 2013; Yost & Thomas, 2012). While bisexual women have been rated as unlikeable, bisexual men have been rated as cruel, dishonest, and irresponsible (Matsuda et al., 2014). Overall, bisexual women tend to be rated less negatively than bisexual men, which has been linked to how women's same-sex sexuality is understood as erotic and sexy, particularly to heterosexual men (Alarie & Gaudet, 2013; Dodge et al., 2016; Yost & Thomas, 2012). Some studies have identified that men may be less tolerant of bisexual people than women are, and less tolerant of bisexual men than of bisexual women (De Bruin & Arndt, 2010; Dodge et al., 2016; Eliason, 1997; Yost & Thomas, 2012). This has sometimes been explained in terms of the threat that same-sex/gender sexuality may present within traditional masculinities, and how this could link to a dislike of (gay and) bisexual men (De Bruin & Arndt, 2010; Yost & Thomas, 2012). However, a recent study found that attitudes towards bisexuality did not differ according to the gender of the perceiver; hence, findings are mixed, and understandings may be changing (Hertlein et al., 2016).

The intersection of bisexuality with race and ethnicity is an important consideration that we know little about (see also Box 3.4). It has been highlighted that people of Colour are likely to experience prejudice and discrimination on the basis of their race and ethnicity and their sex/gender, and sexuality. This is particularly relevant in relation to race-based discrimination from LGBTQ+ communities (which are often made up of mainly White members) and sexuality-based discrimination from within communities of Colour (which may be made up of mainly heterosexual members), alongside other forms of discrimination (e.g., on the basis of gender, and so on) (e.g., Calabrese, Meyer, Overstreet, Haile, & Hansen, 2015; Thompson, 2012; Watson et al., 2019). Demographic data indicates that just over half of bisexual people are people of Colour – a higher figure than in either heterosexual or lesbian and gay populations – and that they are less likely to be out and open about their sexuality (Gates, 2010). However, there are minimal studies on the perceptions or experiences of bisexual people of Colour. In a South African study, there were no significant differences between Black and White students' attitudes to bisexual people (De Bruin & Arndt, 2010). However, US researchers reported that African-American participants had higher scores on a measure of internalised binegativity compared with White participants (Molina et al., 2015).

Studies have shown that younger participants have more positive attitudes towards bisexuality than older people. In one British qualitative study, adolescent bisexual males reported that they felt supported by peers of all sexualities (Morris, McCormack, & Anderson, 2014). Younger bisexual men have also reported almost entirely positive experiences of coming out to friends and family, in contrast to the experiences of older bisexual men (McCormack, Anderson, & Adams, 2014). Findings from various studies indicate that understandings of bisexuality are more generally becoming more positive than they were in the past (e.g., Colledge, Hickson, Reid, & Weatherburn, 2015; McCormack et al., 2014; Morris et al., 2014). Morris et al. (2014) concluded that double discrimination was not evident in their research with young bisexual men. They discussed that this could possibly be due to changing understandings of masculinities, alongside an increasing acceptance of diverse sexualities. This mirrors reports that lesbian and gay sexualities are becoming more accepted, and that homophobia is decreasing within Western cultures (McCormack et al., 2014). However, researchers have been cautious about how findings can be interpreted. Dodge et al. (2016) noted that, while their results did not indicate explicitly negative attitudes towards bisexuality, some participants tended to neither agree nor disagree with statements on Likert scales. This might indicate that participants were ambivalent about bisexuality – perhaps because they did not (knowingly) know any bisexual people – or could be due to social desirability, where participants were not willing to respond in ways that might indicate that they were discriminatory. Some research has continued to identify that bisexual people expect and experience biphobia from friends and family, which informs how out and open they are about their bisexuality (Todd, Oravecz, & Vejar, 2016; Wandrey et al., 2015; see also Chapters 5 and 6).

The impact of bisexual people's experiences of biphobia, bisexual negativity, and bisexual marginalisation

Binegativity contributes significantly to the invisibility of bisexual people, because denigration and dismissal serve to erase bisexuality. There is an ever-increasing body of research which explores bisexual people's experiences of bisexual marginalisation and bisexual invisibility, and the impact this has on them (Box 3.5).

BOX 3.5 MEASURING EXPERIENCES OF BIPHOBIA

Anti-Bisexual Experiences Scale (ABES) (Brewster & Moradi, 2010)

US psychologists Melanie Brewster and Bonnie Moradi developed the ABES. They highlighted that there had been no studies exploring bisexual people's own experiences of prejudice and discrimination in relation to psychological distress. Therefore, they developed the ABES to measure bisexual people's experiences of anti-bisexual prejudice – from heterosexual people (ABES-H) and lesbian and gay people (ABES-LG). Scale items were psychometrically tested based on results from 350 bisexual people. The final scales included 17 items, which fitted into three factors:

1. Sexual orientation instability (e.g., "people have acted as if my bisexuality is only a sexual curiosity, not a stable sexual orientation").
2. Sexual irresponsibility (e.g., "people have treated me as if I am obsessed with sex because I am bisexual").
3. Interpersonal hostility (e.g., "people have not wanted to be my friend because I identify as bisexual") (Brewster & Moradi, 2010, p. 457).

After confirmatory analysis, the scale was retested and validated with a sample of over 175 bisexual participants (Brewster & Moradi, 2010). A group of US researchers have also tested the scale with other identities such as fluid, pansexual, and queer, and with samples which have included trans and cisgender people (Mitchell, Davis, & Galupo, 2015).

The research literature has made links between the prejudice and discrimination that bisexual people experience, and their physical, sexual, and emotional well-being (Mulick & Wright, 2011; Ross et al., 2010). For example, participants who have higher scores on the ABES (see Box 3.5) have lower scores on measures of physical health (Katz-Wise, Mereish, & Woulfe, 2017), psychological well-being (Brewster et al., 2013), and self-esteem (Lambe et al., 2017; Taylor, 2018). Similarly, higher scores on the ABES have been associated with higher scores on measures of psychological distress (Brewster et al., 2013), loneliness (which in turn was linked with psychological distress and suicidality; Mereish, Katz-Wise, & Woulfe, 2017), depression (Lambe et al., 2017), and drug and alcohol use (Watson, Velez, Brownfield, & Flores, 2016). However, findings have been mixed, with researchers also reporting no link between anti-bisexual experiences and mental health or substance use (Bauer, Flanders, MacLeod, & Ross, 2016). Nonetheless, researchers have written of a mental health crisis among bisexual people, perhaps as a result of bisexual marginalisation, on the basis that bisexual participants have commonly been found to have poorer mental health than either heterosexual or lesbian and gay people (Morrison et al., 2016; Ross et al., 2010; see also Taylor, 2018). However, it is particularly important not to pathologise bisexual people further on the basis of their mental well-being (Ross et al., 2010).

It has been suggested that the invalidation and invisibility of bisexuality can result in bisexual people internalising biphobia and questioning the validity of their own identity (Mulick & Wright, 2011). Bisexual marginalisation also impacts on how out and open bisexual people feel able to be. Some younger bisexual women have reported that they identify with alternative identity labels to avoid binegativity (e.g., as pansexual; however, many pansexual people have highlighted that they do *not* use the term pansexual to avoid biphobia; Wandrey et al., 2015). Bisexual people may find it stressful to decide when and whether to conceal or disclose their bisexuality. To conceal bisexuality may impact on their mental health and leave bisexual people fearful of others outing them. To disclose bisexuality may result in increased bisexual marginalisation, which is also linked to poor mental health (see Roberts et al., 2015).

In some studies, "outness" has been linked to experiences of anti-bisexual discrimination (Brewster et al., 2013), whereas in others it has not (Watson et al., 2016). In one study, participants who were "out" to friends scored more highly on the ABES. However, those who reported higher levels of acceptance of their bisexuality from friends and family had *lower* scores on the ABES. This indicates that being "out" might make bisexual people vulnerable to anti-bisexual discrimination, but that if friends and family are perceived to be accepting of bisexuality, this impacts on bisexual people's perceptions of anti-bisexual discrimination (Roberts et al., 2015).

Finally, researchers have identified that prejudice and discrimination can impact on bisexual people's friendships, family relationships, and partner relationships. For example, biphobia may influence the dynamics of bisexual women's friendships, particularly with heterosexual women (Galupo, 2006). Researchers have also reported that bisexual people have unique experiences of romantic relationships. These lived experiences may differ according to sex/gender, partner sex/gender, and type of relationship. Bisexual people may find that potential partners are wary of becoming involved in a relationship with them due to binegativity. They may also have to manage the burden of educating their partners about their bisexuality to address misnomers about them and their identity. For example, bisexual women in relationships with men have sometimes reported that their partners have sexually objectified them in ways associated with common cultural understandings of bisexuality. Further, those who are monogamous may be more likely to feel that they are not "bisexual enough" because they are in a relationship with a person of one sex/gender. Additionally, bisexual people are often assumed to be heterosexual or lesbian/gay on the basis of the sex/gender of their partner. This can be frustrating and leave bisexual people feeling that their bisexuality is disappearing and (extra) invisible to others. Those who are consensually non-monogamous /polyamorous may feel that they are able to "live out" their bisexuality by being in multiple relationships with people of more than one sex/gender. However, to be consensually non-monogamous/polyamorous is no guarantee of visibility, and to be open about these types of relationship models adds an extra layer of complexity because they too are also understood in negative ways (e.g., Dyar, Feinstein, & London, 2014; Hayfield et al., 2018; Klesse, 2005; Li, Dobinson, Scheim, & Ross, 2013; Robinson, 2013).

In summary, cultural understandings of bisexuality serve to deny the existence of bisexuality altogether, or to discredit bisexuality as a credible form of identity, both of which contribute to bisexual invisibility and erasure. Particular nuances have been identified in research studies, which indicate that people's experiences of bisexuality are likely to vary according to a range of factors, including sexuality, gender, race and ethnicity, relationship status, and age. Overall, research indicates that lesbian, gay, and heterosexual people often feel negatively about bisexuality and bisexual people, and that this potentially has a considerable impact on bisexual people's health, well-being, and social relationships.

References

Alarie, M., & Gaudet, S. (2013). "I don't know if she is bisexual or if she just wants to get attention": Analyzing the various mechanisms through which emerging adults invisibilize bisexuality. *Journal of Bisexuality, 13*(2), 191–214. doi:10.1080/15299716.2013.780004

Anderson, E., McCormack, M., & Ripley, M. (2016). Sixth form girls and bisexual burden. *Journal of Gender Studies, 25*(1), 24–34. doi:10.1080/09589236.2013.877383

Armstrong, H. L., & Reissing, E. D. (2014). Attitudes toward casual sex, dating, and committed relationships with bisexual partners. *Journal of Bisexuality, 14*(2), 236–264. doi:10.1080/15299716.2014.902784

Arndt, M., & De Bruin, K. (2011). Measurement of attitudes toward bisexual men and women among South African university students: The validation of an instrument. *Journal of Homosexuality, 58*(4), 497–520. doi:10.1080/00918369.2011.555672

Barker, M., Bowes-Catton, H., Iantaffi, A., Cassidy, A., & Brewer, L. (2008). British bisexuality: A snapshot of bisexual representations and identities in the United Kingdom. *Journal of Bisexuality, 8*(1–2), 141–162. doi:10.1080/15299710802143026

Barker, M., & Langdridge, D. (2010). Whatever happened to non-monogamies? Critical reflections on recent research and theory. *Sexualities, 13*(6), 748–772. doi:10.1177/1363460710384645

Barker, M. J. (2015). Depression and/or oppression? Bisexuality and mental health. *Journal of Bisexuality, 15*(3), 369–384. doi:10.1080/15299716.2014.995853

Bauer, G. R., Flanders, C., MacLeod, M. A., & Ross, L. E. (2016). Occurrence of multiple mental health or substance use outcomes among bisexuals: A respondent-driven sampling study. *BMC Public Health, 16*(1), 497. doi:10.1186/s12889-016-3173-z

Baumgartner, R. (2017). "I think that I'm not a relationship person": Bisexual women's accounts of (internalised) binegativity in non-monogamous relationship narratives. *Psychology and Sexualities Review, 8*(2), 25–40.

Belous, C. K., & Bauman, M. L. (2017). What's in a name? Exploring pansexuality online. *Journal of Bisexuality, 17*(1), 58–72. doi:10.1080/15299716.2016.1224212

Bennett, K. (1992). Feminist bisexuality: A both/and option for an either/or world. In E. R. Weise (Ed.), *Closer to home: Bisexuality and feminism* (pp. 205–231). London: Airlift.

Bradford, M. (2006). Affirmative psychotherapy with bisexual women. *Journal of Bisexuality, 6*(1–2), 13–25. doi:10.1300/J159v06n01_02

Brewster, M. E., & Moradi, B. (2010). Perceived experiences of anti-bisexual prejudice: Instrument development and evaluation. *Journal of Counseling Psychology, 57*(4), 451. doi:10.1037/a0021116

Brewster, M. E., Moradi, B., DeBlaere, C., & Velez, B. L. (2013). Navigating the borderlands: The roles of minority stressors, bicultural self-efficacy, and cognitive flexibility in the mental health of bisexual individuals. *Journal of Counseling Psychology, 60*(4), 543–556. doi:10.1037/a0033224

Brown, M. F., & Lilton, D. L. (2019). Finding the "B" in LGBTQ+: Collections and practices that support the bisexual and pansexual communities. In B. Mehra (Ed.), *LGBTQ+ librarianship in the 21st century: Emerging directions of advocacy and community engagement in diverse information environments* (pp. 143–165). Bingley: Emerald. doi:10.1108/S0065-283020190000045013

Calabrese, S. K., Meyer, I. H., Overstreet, N. M., Haile, R., & Hansen, N. B. (2015). Exploring discrimination and mental health disparities faced by Black sexual minority women using a minority stress framework. *Psychology of Women Quarterly, 39*(3), 287–304. doi:10.1177/0361684314560730

Carrigan, M. (2015). Asexuality. In C. Richards, & M. J. Barker (Eds.), *The Palgrave handbook of sexuality and gender* (pp. 7–23). Basingstoke: Palgrave Macmillan. doi:10.1057/9781137345899_2

Channing, I., & Ward, J. (2017). Homophobia, Brexit and constitutional change. *Safer Communities, 16*(4), 166–175. doi:10.1108/SC-08-2017-0032

Colledge, L., Hickson, F., Reid, D., & Weatherburn, P. (2015). Poorer mental health in UK bisexual women than lesbians: Evidence from the UK 2007 Stonewall women's health survey. *Journal of Public Health, 37*(3), 427–437. doi:10.1093/pubmed/fdu105

Comeau, D. L. (2012). Label-first sexual identity development: An in-depth case study of women who identify as bisexual before having sex with more than one gender. *Journal of Bisexuality, 12*(3), 321–346. doi:10.1080/15299716.2012.702611

De Bruin, K., & Arndt, M. (2010). Attitudes toward bisexual men and women in a university context: Relations with race, gender, knowing a bisexual man or woman and sexual orientation. *Journal of Bisexuality, 10*(3), 233–252. doi:10.1080/15299716.2010.500955

Diamond, L. M. (2005). "I'm straight, but I kissed a girl": The trouble with American media representations of female-female sexuality. *Feminism & Psychology, 15*(1), 104–110. doi:10.1177/0959353505049712

Doan Van, E. E., Mereish, E. H., Woulfe, J. M., & Katz-Wise, S. L. (2019). Perceived discrimination, coping mechanisms, and effects on health in bisexual and other non-monosexual adults. *Archives of Sexual Behavior, 48*(1), 159–174. doi:10.1007/s10508-018-1254-z

Dodge, B., Herbenick, D., Friedman, M. R., Schick, V., Fu, T. C. J., Bostwick, W., … Sandfort, T. G. (2016). Attitudes toward bisexual men and women among a nationally representative probability sample of adults in the United States. *Plos One, 11*, 10. doi:10.1371/journal.pone.0164430

Dyar, C., Feinstein, B. A., & London, B. (2014). Dimensions of sexual identity and minority stress among bisexual women: The role of partner gender. *Psychology of Sexual Orientation and Gender Diversity, 1*(4), 441–452. doi:10.1037/sgd0000063

Eisner, S. (2013). *Bi: Notes for a bisexual revolution.* Berkeley: Seal Press.

Eliason, M. (2000). Bi-negativity: The stigma facing bisexual men. *Journal of Bisexuality, 1*(2–3), 137–154. doi:10.1300/J159v01n02_05

Eliason, M., & Elia, J. P. (2011). Reflections about bisexuality and the *Journal of Bisexuality. Journal of Bisexuality, 11*(4), 412–419. doi:10.1080/15299716.2011.620463

Eliason, M. J. (1997). The prevalence and nature of biphobia in heterosexual undergraduate students. *Archives of Sexual Behavior, 26*(3), 317–326. doi:10.1023/A:1024527032040

Fahs, B. (2009). Compulsory bisexuality? The challenges of modern sexual fluidity. *Journal of Bisexuality, 9*(3–4), 431–449. doi:10.1080/15299710903316661

Farhall, K. (2018). "Girl-on-girl confessions!" Changing representations of female-female sexuality in two Australian women's magazines. *Sexualities, 21*(1–2), 212–232. doi:10.1177/1363460716679388

Formby, E. (2013). Understanding and responding to homophobia and bullying: Contrasting staff and young people's views within community settings in England. *Sexuality Research and Social Policy*, *10*(4), 302–316. doi:10.1007/s13178-013-0135-4

Friedman, M. R., Dodge, B., Schick, V., Herbenick, D., Hubach, R. D., Bowling, J., ... Reece, M. (2014). From bias to bisexual health disparities: Attitudes toward bisexual men and women in the United States. *LGBT Health*, *1*(4), 309–318. doi:10.1089/lgbt.2014.0005

Friedman, M. R., Stall, R., Plankey, M., Shoptaw, S., Herrick, A. L., Surkan, P. J., ... Silvestre, A. J. (2017). Stability of bisexual behavior and extent of viral bridging behavior among men who have sex with men and women. *Archives of Sexual Behavior*, *46*(4), 903–912. doi:10.1007/s10508-016-0863-7

Galupo, M. P. (2006). Sexism, heterosexism, and biphobia: The framing of bisexual women's friendships. *Journal of Bisexuality*, *6*(3), 35–45. doi:10.1300/J159v06n03_03

Gates, G. J. (2010). *Sexual minorities in the 2008 General Social Survey: Coming out and demographic characteristics.* Los Angeles: UCLA School of Law.

Gonel, A. H. (2013). Pansexual identification in online communities: Employing a collaborative queer method to study pansexuality. *Graduate Journal of Social Science*, *10*(1), 36–59.

Grunt-Mejer, K., & Campbell, C. (2016). Around consensual nonmonogamies: Assessing attitudes toward nonexclusive relationships. *The Journal of Sex Research*, *53*(1), 45–53. doi:10.1080/00224499.2015.1010193

Gupta, K. (2017). "And now I'm just different, but there's nothing actually wrong with me": Asexual marginalization and resistance. *Journal of Homosexuality*, *64*(8), 991–1013. doi:10.1080/00918369.2016.1236590

Hayfield, N., Campbell, C., & Reed, E. (2018). Misrecognition and managing marginalisation: Bisexual people's experiences of bisexuality and relationships. *Psychology & Sexuality*, *9*(3), 221–236. doi:10.1080/19419899.2018.1470106

Hayfield, N., Clarke, V., & Halliwell, E. (2014). Bisexual women's understandings of social marginalisation: "The heterosexuals don't understand us but nor do the lesbians". *Feminism & Psychology*, *24*(3), 352–372. doi:10.1177/0959353514539651

Hemmings, C. (2002). *Bisexual spaces: A geography of sexuality and gender.* London: Routledge.

Herek, G. M. (1984). Beyond "homophobia": A social psychological perspective on attitudes toward lesbians and gay men. *Journal of Homosexuality*, *10*(1–2), 1–21. doi:10.1300/J082v10n01_01

Herek, G. M. (Ed.). (1998). *Stigma and sexual orientation: Understanding prejudice against lesbians, gay men, and bisexuals.* London: Sage.

Herek, G. M. (2004). Beyond "homophobia": Thinking about sexual prejudice and stigma in the twenty-first century. *Sexuality Research & Social Policy*, *1*(2), 6–24. doi:10.1525/srsp.2004.1.2.6

Herek, G. M. (2015). Beyond "homophobia": Thinking more clearly about stigma, prejudice, and sexual orientation. *American Journal of Orthopsychiatry*, *85*(5S), S29. doi:10.1037/ort0000092

Hertlein, K. M., Hartwell, E. E., & Munns, M. E. (2016). Attitudes toward bisexuality according to sexual orientation and gender. *Journal of Bisexuality*, *16*(3), 339–360. doi:10.1080/15299716.2016.1200510

Israel, T., & Mohr, J. J. (2004). Attitudes toward bisexual women and men: Current research, future directions. *Journal of Bisexuality*, *4*(1–2), 117–134. doi:10.1300/J159v04n01_09

Kasl, C. S. (2002). Special issues in counseling lesbian women for sexual addiction, compulsivity, and sexual codependency. *Sexual Addiction &compulsivity: The Journal of Treatment and Prevention, 9*(4), 191–208. doi:10.1080/10720160216044

Katz-Wise, S. L., Mereish, E. H., & Woulfe, J. (2017). Associations of bisexual-specific minority stress and health among cisgender and transgender adults with bisexual orientation. *Journal of Sex Research, 54*(7), 899–910. doi:10.1080/00224499.2016.1236181

Kitzinger, C. (1987). *The social construction of lesbianism*. London: Sage.

Kitzinger, C., & Perkins, R. (1993). *Changing our minds: Lesbian feminism and psychology*. New York: New York University Press.

Klesse, C. (2005). Bisexual women, non-monogamy and differentialist anti-promiscuity discourses. *Sexualities, 8*(4), 445–464. doi:10.1177/1363460705056620

Klesse, C. (2011). Shady characters, untrustworthy partners, and promiscuous sluts: Creating bisexual intimacies in the face of heteronormativity and biphobia. *Journal of Bisexuality, 11*(2–3), 227–244. doi:10.1080/15299716.2011.571987

Lambe, J., Cerezo, A., & O'Shaughnessy, T. (2017). Minority stress, community involvement, and mental health among bisexual women. *Psychology of Sexual Orientation and Gender Diversity, 4*(2), 218–226. doi:10.1037/sgd0000222

Lapointe, A. A. (2017). "It's not pans, it's people": Student and teacher perspectives on bisexuality and pansexuality. *Journal of Bisexuality, 17*(1), 88–107. doi:10.1080/15299716.2016.1196157

Li, T., Dobinson, C., Scheim, A. I., & Ross, L. E. (2013). Unique issues bisexual people face in intimate relationships: A descriptive exploration of lived experience. *Journal of Gay & Lesbian Mental Health, 17*(1), 21–39. doi:10.1080/19359705.2012.723607

Lytle, A., Dyar, C., Levy, S. R., & London, B. (2017). Contact with bisexual individuals reduces binegativity among heterosexuals and lesbian women and gay men. *European Journal of Social Psychology, 47*(5), 580–599. doi:10.1002/ejsp.2241

MacDonald, A. P. (1976). Homophobia: Its roots and meanings. *Homosexual Counseling Journal, 3*(1), 23–33.

Matsuda, W. T., Rouse, S. V., & Miller-Perrin, C. L. (2014). Validation of the attitudes regarding bisexuality scale: Correlations with ratings of a positive media image of bisexual men and women. *Journal of Bisexuality, 14*(2), 265–276. doi:10.1080/15299716.2014.903219

McCormack, M., Anderson, E., & Adams, A. (2014). Cohort effect on the coming out experiences of bisexual men. *Sociology, 48*(6), 1207–1223. doi:10.1177/0038038513518851

McLean, K. (2007). Hiding in the closet? Bisexuals, coming out and the disclosure imperative. *Journal of Sociology, 43*(2), 151–166. doi:10.1177/1440783307076893

McLean, K. (2008a). Inside, outside, nowhere: Bisexual men and women in the gay and lesbian community. *Journal of Bisexuality, 8*(1–2), 63–80. doi:10.1080/15299710802143174

McLean, K. (2008b). Silences and stereotypes: The impact of (mis)constructions of bisexuality on Australian bisexual men and women. *Gay & Lesbian Issues and Psychology Review, 4*(3), 158–165.

Mereish, E. H., Katz-Wise, S. L., & Woulfe, J. (2017). Bisexual-specific minority stressors, psychological distress, and suicidality in bisexual individuals: The mediating role of loneliness. *Prevention Science, 18*(6), 716–725. doi:10.1007/s11121-017-0804-2

Mitchell, R. C., Davis, K. S., & Galupo, M. P. (2015). Comparing perceived experiences of prejudice among self-identified plurisexual individuals. *Psychology & Sexuality, 6*(3), 245–257. doi:10.1080/19419899.2014.940372

Mohr, J. J., & Rochlen, A. B. (1999). Measuring attitudes regarding bisexuality in lesbian, gay male, and heterosexual populations. *Journal of Counseling Psychology, 46*(3), 353–369. doi:10.1037/0022-0167.46.3.353

Molina, Y., Marquez, J. H., Logan, D. E., Leeson, C. J., Balsam, K. F., & Kaysen, D. L. (2015). Current intimate relationship status, depression, and alcohol use among bisexual women: The mediating roles of bisexual-specific minority stressors. *Sex Roles*, *73*(1–2), 43–57. doi:10.1007/s11199-015-0483-z

Morris, M., McCormack, M., & Anderson, E. (2014). The changing experiences of bisexual male adolescents. *Gender and Education*, *26*(4), 397–413. doi:10.1080/09540253.2014.927834

Morrison, K. E., Gruenhage, J. M., & Pedersen, C. L. (2016). Challenging binaries by saying good bi: Perceptions of bisexual men's identity legitimacy. *Journal of Bisexuality*, *16*(3), 361–377. doi:10.1080/15299716.2016.1183157

Morrow, S. L. (2000). First do no harm: Therapist issues in psychotherapy with lesbian, gay, and bisexual clients. In R. M. Perez, K. A. DeBord, & K. J. Bieschke (Eds.), *Handbook of counseling and psychotherapy with lesbian, gay, and bisexual clients* (pp. 137–156). Washington, DC: American Psychological Association. doi:10.1037/10339-006

Mulick, P. S., & Wright, L. W. (2002). Examining the existence of biphobia in the heterosexual and homosexual populations. *Journal of Bisexuality*, *2*(4), 47–64. doi:10.1300/J159v02n04_03

Mulick, P. S., & Wright, L. W. (2011). The biphobia scale a decade later: Reflections and additions. *Journal of Bisexuality*, *11*(4), 453–457. doi:10.1080/15299716.2011.620486

Niki, D. (2018). Now you see me, now you don't: Addressing bisexual invisibility in relationship therapy. *Sexual and Relationship Therapy*, *33*(1–2), 45–57. doi:10.1080/14681994.2017.1419563

Ochs, R. (1996). Biphobia: It goes more than two ways. In B. A. Firestein (Ed.), *Bisexuality: The psychology and politics of an invisible minority* (pp. 217–239). London: Sage.

Ritchie, A., & Barker, M. (2006). "There aren't words for what we do or how we feel so we have to make them up": Constructing polyamorous languages in a culture of compulsory monogamy. *Sexualities*, *9*(5), 584–601. doi:10.1177/1363460706069987

Roberts, T. S., Horne, S. G., & Hoyt, W. T. (2015). Between a gay and a straight place: Bisexual individuals' experiences with monosexism. *Journal of Bisexuality*, *15*(4), 554–569. doi:10.1080/15299716.2015.1111183

Robinson, M. (2013). Polyamory and monogamy as strategic identities. *Journal of Bisexuality*, *13*(1), 21–38. doi:10.1080/15299716.2013.755731

Rosenberg, A., Gates, A., Richmond, K., & Sinno, S. (2017). It's not a joke: Masculinity ideology and homophobic language. *Psychology of Men & Masculinity*, *18*(4), 293–300. doi:10.1037/men0000063

Ross, L. E., Dobinson, C., & Eady, A. (2010). Perceived determinants of mental health for bisexual people: A qualitative examination. *American Journal of Public Health*, *100*(3), 496–502. doi:10.2105/AJPH.2008.156307

Rupp, L. J., & Taylor, V. (2010). Straight girls kissing. *Contexts*, *9*(3), 28–32. doi:10.1525/ctx.2010.9.3.28

Rust, P. C. (1995). *Bisexuality and the challenge to lesbian politics: Sex, loyalty and revolution*. London: New York University Press.

Shabazz, N. (1979). Homophobia: Myths and realities. *Heresies*, *2*(4), 34–36.

Smith, K. T. (1971). Homophobia: A tentative personality profile. *Psychological Reports*, *29*(3.2), 1091–1094. doi:10.2466/pr0.1971.29.3f.1091

Spalding, L. R., & Peplau, L. A. (1997). The unfaithful lover: Heterosexuals' perceptions of bisexuals and their relationships. *Psychology of Women Quarterly*, *21*(4), 611–624. doi:10.1111/j.1471-6402.1997.tb00134.x

Speer, S. A., & Potter, J. (2000). The management of heterosexist talk: Conversational resources and prejudiced claims. *Discourse & Society*, *11*(4), 543–572. doi:10.1177/0957926500011004005

Taylor, J. (2018). Bisexual mental health: A call to action. *Issues in Mental Health Nursing*, *39*(1), 83–92. doi:10.1080/01612840.2017.1391904

Thompson, B. Y. (2012). The price of "community" from bisexual/biracial women's perspectives. *Journal of Bisexuality*, *12*(3), 417–428. doi:10.1080/15299716.2012.702623

Todd, M. E., Oravecz, L., & Vejar, C. (2016). Biphobia in the family context: Experiences and perceptions of bisexual individuals. *Journal of Bisexuality*, *16*(2), 144–162. doi:10.1080/15299716.2016.1165781

Tully, C., & Albro, J. C. (1979). Homosexuality: A social worker's imbroglio. *Journal of Sociology and Social Welfare*, *6*(2), 154–167.

Wandrey, R. L., Mosack, K. E., & Moore, E. M. (2015). Coming out to family and friends as bisexually identified young adult women: A discussion of homophobia, biphobia, and heteronormativity. *Journal of Bisexuality*, *15*(2), 204–229. doi:10.1080/15299716.2015.1018657

Warwick, I., & Aggleton, P. (2014). Bullying, "cussing" and "mucking about": Complexities in tackling homophobia in three secondary schools in south London, UK. *Sex Education*, *14*(2), 159–173. doi:10.1080/14681811.2013.854204

Watson, L. B., Velez, B. L., Brownfield, J., & Flores, M. J. (2016). Minority stress and bisexual women's disordered eating: The role of maladaptive coping. *Counseling Psychologist*, *44*(8), 1158–1186. doi:10.1177/0011000016669233

Watson, R. J., Allen, A., Pollitt, A. M., & Eaton, L. A. (2019). Risk and protective factors for sexual health outcomes among black bisexual men in the US: Internalized heterosexism, sexual orientation disclosure, and religiosity. *Archives of Sexual Behavior*, *48*(1), 243–253. doi:10.1007/s10508-018-1216-5

Weinberg, G. H. (1972). *Society and the healthy homosexual*. New York: Macmillan.

Wilkinson, S. (1996). Bisexuality "a la mode". *Women's Studies International Forum*, *19*(3), 293–301. doi:10.1016/0277-5395(96)00016-7

Yost, M. R., & Thomas, G. D. (2012). Gender and binegativity: Men's and women's attitudes toward male and female bisexuals. *Archives of Sexual Behavior*, *41*(3), 691–702. doi:10.1007/s10508-011-9767-8

Zivony, A., & Saguy, T. (2018). Stereotype deduction about bisexual women. *Journal of Sex Research*, *55*(4–5), 666–678. doi:10.1080/00224499.2018.1437116

4

IN/VISIBLE VISUAL IDENTITIES

How we look can be understood as a visual identity which reflects aspects of our wider social and cultural identities, and which can therefore make us visible to others. Accordingly, people can potentially express and communicate their identities through their dress and appearance, including clothing, hair, make-up, jewellery, and other adornments (Hayfield, 2013). If someone says the words Goth, emo, mod, punk, or hippy, for example, we can conjure a visual image in our mind of what someone who identifies with these subcultural identities might look like (Box 4.1). Across the life-span, our demographic identities, such as our race and ethnicity, age, social class, sex/gender, and sexuality, can be revealed (or in some cases, strategically concealed) through how we look (Franklin, 2001; Halim, Gutierrez, Bryant, Arredondo, & Takesako, 2018; Hollingworth & Williams, 2009; Jankowski, Diedrichs, Williamson, Christopher, & Harcourt, 2016; Taylor, 2007, 2008; Twigg, 2007; Ylänne, 2012). However, psychologists have tended to overlook the importance of appearance and how it interlinks with our identities (Halim et al., 2018). The result is that there is minimal psychological research around appearance and how it relates to our personal, social, and cultural identities (and distinctions between these may be blurry). Despite this, some psychologists – and sociologists, cultural studies scholars, and those in other social science disciplines – have recognised the importance of sexuality, appearance, and visual identities. This chapter focuses on the existence and functions of lesbian and gay visual identities in contrast to the lack of distinctive bisexual, pansexual, asexual, and plurisexual visual identities.

BOX 4.1 SUBCULTURAL VISUAL IDENTITIES

Within a range of subcultures, shared appearance – including what is worn, and how it is worn – can enable expression of social identity and signal belonging within associated social groups (Polhemus, 1996). Many of these visual identities represent a rejection of mainstream culture, and blur the lines between (traditional notions of) masculinity and femininity.

Goth

Goth identities link closely with musical preferences and developed during the post-punk era, most notably in the UK and US. Goth visual identities are wide-ranging (e.g., old school, cybergoth, steampunk), but often include flamboyant dress in the form of lace, silk, velvet, or leather clothing, corsets, waistcoats, top hats, tail coats, piercings, and elaborate jewellery and make-up. Goth looks are often sombre, through the dominance of black clothing, (dyed) dark hair, and nail varnish, regardless of gender. Scholars have argued that Goth dress and appearance represent non-conformity and defiance of cultural and gendered norms (Brill, 2008; van Elferen & Weinstock, 2016; Widdicombe & Wooffitt, 1995).

Hippy

Hippies are often associated with the 1960s/1970s free-love era. A key aspect of hippy identities was dropping out of mainstream society and resisting consumerism and fashion. Consequently, hippy looks were based on the "natural", including wearing (often patchwork) colours which appear in nature, such as browns, greens, and blues. Hippies wore loose clothing such as ponchos, long skirts, bell-bottom trousers, or flared jeans, with sandals, beads, and headbands. There was a blurring of lines between genders, with hippies of all genders often having long hair and similar styles of clothing (Tierney, 2017; Welters, 2008).

Flyboys and flygirls/b-boys and b-girls

Flyboys and flygirls (or b-boys and b-girls) appeared primarily in New York during the 1970s within Black hip hop communities. Flyboy looks have changed over time, but have included casual oversized clothing such as hoodies, sweatpants, or baggy jeans, and brand-name clothes, such as Puma or Nike trainers (with fat laces), Adidas tracksuits or jogging bottoms and T-shirts, large Cazal glasses, and Kangol baseball caps, have been popular. Flygirls have sometimes shared similar looks, but have also been associated with short skirts, bra tops, and large gold jewellery. Hairstyles have ranged from shaved heads to plaits or dreadlocks. These looks have spread outside Black communities as hip hop has become popular (Lewis, 2010).

Appearance, sexuality, and visual identities

Sociologist Erving Goffman argued that we observe those around us and then construct ourselves in order to manage the impressions that others might have of us (Goffman, 1959/1990). When we present ourselves through our appearance, others are able to interpret (their understandings of) what this indicates about our personal, social, and cultural identities (Gleeson & Frith, 2003; Hethorn & Kaiser, 1998). Our identities can, in effect, be worn upon the body, and so appearance becomes a reflection of, or a "kind of visual metaphor" for, our identities (Davis, 1992, p. 25; see also Halim et al., 2018; Hancock, Strübel, Peirson-Smith, & Nishida, 2017). Mutual recognition of shared identity, on the basis of self-presentation, can be understood as a form of friendly social inter-action. Recognition may lead to a nod or a smile, whereas to not be acknow-ledged can leave us feeling overlooked, disregarded, and as though we are "not worthy of a glance" (Goffman, 1963, p. 83). Of course, there are some com-plexities in the idea of appearance as a conduit for communicating our identities to others in the wider world. Appearance can be used as a tool to blend in or stand out, but we cannot choose *not* to appear (Frith & Gleeson, 2003; Hancock et al., 2017). Therefore, we cannot opt out of having a visual identity and we are likely to be read from our appearance whether we intend to be or not (Han-cock et al., 2017; Todd & Funder, 2016). Although we may express our iden-tities (including our sexualities) through our dress and appearance, we cannot assume that others will always "read" or perceive us in a way that corresponds with our intentions (Daly, King, & Yeadon-Lee, 2018; Hartman, 2013; Hethorn & Kaiser, 1998; Kaiser, 2012). However, there is some evidence that sexuality may be read accurately by others on the basis of appearance alongside other non-verbal cues (Todd & Funder, 2016). Communicating through appearance may also be context-dependent, according to the (limits of) the space we are in, who else occupies that space, and whether they will understand our visual lan-guage (Hethorn & Kaiser, 1998; Reddy-Best & Pedersen, 2015). Nonetheless, appearance potentially serves as a non-verbal communication tool to convey information about us to others, as well as historically having served particular functions (Clarke & Smith, 2015; Daly et al., 2018; Davis, 1992; Todd & Funder, 2016).

Expressing self and sexuality

Research has identified that when lesbian and gay people first "realise" their sexual identity, they may alter their appearance to adhere to recognisable lesbian and gay visual identities (Box 4.2). Therefore, lesbian and gay people can express their sexuality through a range of appearance norms in order to convey, and take pride in, their sexual identity. To "dress the part" can allow lesbian and gay people to resist the (gendered) dress codes of (hegemonic and heteronormative) heterosexual society and take pleasure in feeling "comfortable" and able to express their "real selves" (Barry & Martin, 2016; Clarke & Smith, 2015; Clarke & Spence, 2013; Clarke & Turner, 2007; Holliday, 1999; Hutson, 2010; Huxley, Clarke, & Halliwell, 2014; Kaiser, 1998, 2012; Levitt & Hiestand, 2005; Myers, Taub, Morris, & Rothblum, 1999; Reddy-Best & Pedersen, 2015). When lesbian and gay people modify their appearance in order to "look the part", they may stand out from heterosexual mainstream society. Indeed, a contrast between the social identities with which we identify and those with which we do not is a critical part of claiming and embracing identity (Clarke & Smith, 2015; Clarke & Turner, 2007; Daly et al., 2018; Hutson, 2010; Huxley et al., 2014; Polhemus, 1996).

BOX 4.2 LESBIAN AND GAY VISUAL IDENTITIES

The most recognisable images of lesbian and gay people rely on notions of gender inversion (see Chapter 2). Hence, lesbians have often been associated with masculinity and gay men with femininity (Barry & Martin, 2016; Clarke & Turner, 2007; Hayfield, 2013; Hayfield, Clarke, Halliwell, & Malson, 2013; Kaiser, 2012; Todd & Funder, 2016).

Perhaps the most commonly understood visual images of lesbians are butch and femme. The butch look is the most documented and recognised. It encompasses elements of appearance often associated with masculinity (some butch lesbians do not necessarily associate *themselves* with notions of masculinity, although others might). Butch looks include short hair (cut and styled in particular ways), "sensible" or comfortable shoes, "masculine" clothing and mannerisms, and particular (placements of) jewellery, tattoos, and piercings (Clarke & Turner, 2007; Esterberg, 1996; Krakauer & Rose, 2002; Myers et al., 1999; Reddy-Best & Pedersen, 2015; Rothblum, 1994, 2010). Femme looks may be somewhat less visible than butch looks but have a rich history within lesbian cultures. Femme lesbians tend to embrace more traditionally feminine appearance, including make-up, dresses, or skirts, which may well mean that their identity is somewhat invisible if they are assumed to be heterosexual (Luzzatto & Gvion, 2004; Rothblum, 2010).

The most commonly recognised visual image of gay men is of the camp and trendy effeminate gay man. This look is based on notions more traditionally linked to femininity, such as bright, tight, and fashionable (sometimes branded) clothing and accessories. Gay men have also been associated with grooming practices such as dying and styling their hair. This type of image is closely associated with the idea that gay men are highly invested in how they look and likely to devote time and money to their dress and appearance in ways more traditionally associated with heterosexual women (Clarke & Smith, 2015; Clarke & Turner, 2007; Cole, 2019; Hayfield, 2013; Hutson, 2010). A range of hypermasculine (and sometimes hypermuscular) looks and styles also exist for gay men (Cole, 2019; Hutson, 2010). Indeed, lesbian and gay looks are plural rather than monolithic and a diverse range of nuanced and ever-changing specific looks and styles, many of which do not fit with notions of masculine women and effeminate men, may also be embraced (Barry & Martin, 2016; Clarke & Turner, 2007; Cole, 2019; Hayfield et al., 2013; Kaiser, 2012).

Some researchers have meaningfully included bisexual men and women in their wider studies of lesbian, gay, and bisexual appearance (Clarke & Smith, 2015; Clarke & Turner, 2007; Hayfield, 2013; Holliday, 1999; Huxley et al., 2014; Rothblum, 2010). A few scholars have specifically sought to understand bisexual appearance and focused on (the lack of) bisexual looks, primarily in relation to bisexual women (Brennan, 2011; Brennan & Behrensen, 2012; Daly et al., 2018; Hartman, 2013; Hayfield et al., 2013; Taub, 1999). However, there is far from a clear picture of bisexual visual identities, and to date pansexual, asexual, and plurisexual identities have been overlooked within the appearance literature. Due to the minimal theory, research, or understanding about appearance and visual identities, this chapter is limited to discussions of bisexuality, although some of the ideas discussed here could potentially be extended to pansexual, asexual, and plurisexual identities.

The in/visibility of bisexual people

In this section I use selected quotations from participants who took part in my, Victoria Clarke, Emma Halliwell, and Helen Malson's study on bisexuality and appearance (for details of the sample, see Chapter 1; for the full results, see Hayfield et al., 2013). When participants in the study were asked directly about bisexual dress and appearance, they struggled to discuss the topic and concluded that there were no recognisable looks for bisexual people:

> I don't *know* many people who are bisexual so … I can't build up an image in my head of bisexuality […] there's very few people who are out there as bisexual.
>
> *(Roxy)*

> I've never even thought about "oh bisexual look" because the way I've always done it is "gay going out on the scene, straight going out with David [partner]" (*laughs*) as opposed to "bisexual".
>
> *(Elizabeth)*

Roxy linked the lack of bisexual visual images to the lack of bisexual visibility more widely, whereas Elizabeth had not contemplated the possibility of a bisexual look until she took part in the research. These narratives indicate that a bisexual look cannot be talked about because, unlike lesbian and gay looks, bisexual looks do not exist, and bisexual people cannot be seen (Hayfield et al., 2013). Other researchers have also identified a lack of recognisable bisexual appearance norms or dress codes (Clarke & Turner, 2007; Daly et al., 2018; Hayfield, 2013; Hayfield et al., 2013; Hayfield & Wood, 2019; Huxley et al., 2014; Taub, 1999). The absence of bisexual looks (at least among these mainly White British and US bisexual participants) serves as an example of how these bisexual people are seemingly physically invisible, both to each other and to other people. This lack of clear bisexual (and pansexual, asexual, and plurisexual) visual identities means that they are far less likely to have the option of meaningfully expressing their bisexuality through their dress and appearance in the ways that lesbian and gay people may be able to (Hayfield et al., 2013).

Being identifiable and identifying others

Through their *shared* visual identities, lesbian and gay people (and perhaps those who identify more broadly as queer) are able to be "out" and become visible to others (Clarke & Smith, 2015; Reddy-Best & Pedersen, 2015). Therefore, appearance norms can act as a form of signalling and enable the recognition of others who are "like us", which in turn can create a sense of solidarity. Appearance can also serve to reject the gaze of men and attract women (for lesbians), or to reject the gaze of women and attract men (for gay men) (e.g., Cole, 2000; Esterberg, 1996; Krakauer & Rose, 2002; Levitt & Hiestand, 2005; Luzzatto & Gvion, 2004; Rothblum, 1994). However, this is more complex for bisexual, pansexual, and plurisexual people, and those with asexual spectrum identities which relate to attraction to more than one gender, who are not likely to want to reject the gaze of any one gender, yet may find it difficult to convey their attraction to multiple genders through their appearance (see also Box 4.3, below).

Lesbian and gay appearance can be subtle, particularly when it is about not only *what* is worn, but also *how* it is worn (Kaiser, 1998). Some appearance norms may allow lesbian and gay people to identify each other without being identifiable to the wider heterosexual culture. This was particularly important in the past when "homosexual acts" were illegal, and when widespread homophobia required high levels of discretion about sexuality (Clarke & Turner, 2007; Cole, 2000; Krakauer & Rose, 2002). Bisexual (and pansexual, asexual, or plurisexual) people may have sufficient insider knowledge to recognise lesbian and gay appearance, in particular butch lesbians and effeminate gay men (Clarke & Smith, 2015; Clarke & Spence, 2013; Rothblum, 2010). Some research participants have suggested that such images may be one-dimensional and based at least in part on media mis/representations (Clarke & Smith, 2015; Daly et al., 2018). However, bisexual research participants have reported that they initially dismissed butch looks as stereotypes, only to find that these were visible on "the scene" (Clarke & Spence, 2013). In the appearance study (Hayfield et al., 2013), bisexual women described how a lesbian was recognisable when she was "more like a man" (Amy) and had "the really manly kind of look" (Blue). Others spoke about appearance in a way which indicated that they understood lesbian identities as embodied. Marie discussed how one particular lesbian she knew "made it very obvious, even in the way she'd stand, and the way she walked, so it was like almost a swagger which I found quite common with a lot of lesbians". Another participant described "the confident, butch lesbian and that's how they walk and do their swagger" (Emily) (Hayfield et al., 2013). A "lesbian walk" or "swagger" conjures a confident assertion of lesbian identity, and is one way in which lesbian appearance can make identity recognisable to others (Esterberg, 1996).

In their discussions of lesbian looks, the bisexual women in our study created a picture of a visible lesbian identity through a combination of clothes, hairstyles, and embodiment of sexuality. This demonstrates how lesbians may become recognisable not only to other lesbians, but also to bisexual (and perhaps pansexual, asexual, and plurisexual) people (Clarke & Spence, 2013; Daly et al., 2018; Hutson, 2010). Other research has identified that heterosexual research participants are similarly able to describe particular images of lesbians and gay men often on the basis of gender inversion, although they too have tended to dismiss these as stereotypes (e.g., Hayfield, 2013; Peel, 2005).

Non-identifiable bisexuality

While some lesbian and gay looks may be recognisable to others, bisexuality is seemingly non-identifiable due to a lack of distinctive bisexual looks (Clarke & Turner, 2007; Hayfield, 2013; Hayfield et al., 2013; Hayfield & Wood, 2019; Huxley et al., 2014; Taub, 1999). In the appearance study, participants were specifically asked whether they could recognise bisexuality through appearance. They often answered by discussing the recognisability of lesbian identities, in stark contrast to the imperceptibility of bisexual identities:

> I think I always forget that people might be bi (*laughs*) [...] I do still think "oh that person, they look a bit like a lesbian". And then I might come back from that and think "ooh they might be bisexual" but it's not a sort of instinctive "a ha! You have that look".
>
> *(Eddy)*

The lack of bisexual looks and the associated lack of recognition of bisexuality has also been identified in other research with lesbian, gay, heterosexual, and bisexual participants (see Box 4.3, below). Appearance seemingly cannot serve as a communication tool to convey bisexual (or pansexual, asexual, and plurisexual) identities in the way it potentially can for those with lesbian and gay (and to some extent heterosexual) identities (Hayfield, 2013; Hayfield et al., 2013). Instead, for bisexual people to come out they have to explicitly state their sexuality:

> I think more than anything it'll come up in *how* I talk, or what I talk about, more likely than through my image.
>
> *(Lucy)*

> If you want to be visible as a bisexual it's usually a verbal thing, you have to do the declaration of coming out, rather than the more subtle communications […] I'm extraordinarily resistant to noticing (*laughs*) that other people are bi […] and it's not until somebody actually hits me round the head with a large stick that I realise that people are bi … I don't know if you'd call that invisible or just cluelessness.
>
> *(Eddy)*

Eddy locates her inability to recognise other bisexual people as due to her "cluelessness". However, a lack of ability to recognise bisexuality could instead be attributed to the lack of bisexual visual identities alongside the wider lack of bisexual visibility within Western cultures. This indicates that people are unlikely to be able to convey their attraction to more than one sex/gender – particularly when sexuality is understood only as a mixture of lesbian/gay and heterosexual identities and therefore in binary terms, which excludes bisexual (and pansexual, asexual, and plurisexual) people (Daly et al., 2018; Hayfield et al., 2013). The lack of bisexual visual identities means that bisexual (and perhaps pansexual, asexual, and plurisexual) people are unlikely to be able to come out through their appearance or communicate their bisexuality to others. Instead, the only way in which they can come out is by explicitly stating their sexuality (Hayfield et al., 2013; Maliepaard, 2018).

Creating and consolidating communities

Shared appearance norms have enabled lesbian and gay people to find, and be found by, others who are also lesbian and gay (e.g., Barry & Martin, 2016; Cole, 2000; Esterberg, 1996; Holliday, 1999; Krakauer & Rose, 2002; Reddy-Best & Pedersen, 2015; Rothblum, 1994). Therefore, appearance norms have aided in the creation of coherent lesbian and gay communities (of which bisexual, pansexual, asexual, plurisexual, and trans people are also often a part) (Luzzatto & Gvion, 2004). Within these communities, lesbian and gay people may feel a sense of acceptance and belonging (Daly et al., 2018). These have historically been safe spaces away from the gaze of voyeuristic or homophobic individuals; hence appearance can serve as an indicator of who "belongs", which can help keep these spaces free from outsiders (Cole, 2000; Krakauer & Rose, 2002; Rothblum, 1994). It is within lesbian and gay (and bisexual and trans) spaces such as the commercialised club scene and at Pride events that appearance norms are most commonly situated (Luzzatto & Gvion, 2004; Reddy-Best & Pedersen, 2015; Rothblum, 1994). Accordingly, bisexual participants in the appearance study who went out on the scene reported recognising a variety of nuanced (butch) looks. Berni discussed "bulls" (bulldykes) and "baby dykes", while Blue mentioned the "stone dyke" and the "trendy androgynous dyke" (Hayfield et al., 2013). Bisexual women in previous studies have also been able to identify other nuanced lesbian looks, such as "old school", "sporty", and "biker dyke" lesbians (Clarke & Turner, 2007, p. 270). However, bisexual people do not have their own appearance norms, and have sometimes reported that they do not feel welcome within LGBTQ+ spaces to the extent that they may not be out about their bisexual identities when on the scene (Hayfield et al., 2013).

Bisexual looks in bisexual communities (and beyond)?

While bisexuality may not be associated with distinctive or identifiable bisexual images, participants in research studies have reported that there may be elements of shared alternative appearances, particularly within bisexual spaces (Hayfield, 2013; Hayfield et al., 2013; Huxley et al., 2014). In the appearance study, this included Goth looks. Claire stated: "if you asked me what I think would be a very visible look, I would say Goth on the bisexual scene is a big look". Ruth reported that when she attended BiCon (the largest UK national bisexual gathering; see Chapter 6), "there were loads of people who I would broadly classify as Goth". For Adele, "the one look that I've seen the most [at BiCon] has been a Goth sort of look". Participants also discussed other alternative looks. For example, when Claire was asked whether she might be able to identify other people as bisexual:

> I think I sometimes do. And I think that I also successfully read people as alternative and I think that a lot of what bi people do [...] is that they look a bit alternative, so if someone's got a nose ring, or someone's got dyed hair, or multiple piercings or tattoos or ... something interesting that reads a bit alternative about the way they look.
>
> *(Claire)*

Ruth also identified a range of subcultural appearances that could potentially be linked with bisexuality:

> I'd be more likely to assume that people who look like Goths, or skaters, or emos, or the kind of ... hippy indie rock end of the young people's cultural spectrum. I'd think it was more likely that they would be bi.
>
> *(Ruth)*

Other research has identified similar findings; for example, a bisexual man suggested that beards and tie-dye clothes may be associated with men in bisexual communities (Holliday, 1999). These alternative looks and identities may function in similar ways to shared appearance within other subcultural groups, providing a sense of safety and solidarity. However, outside bisexual spaces, alternative looks may be associated with multiple meanings across a whole range of identities. Hence these looks are borrowed, or shared, rather than exclusively belonging to bisexual people. Further, in the appearance study (Hayfield et al.,

2013), it was mainly the participants who were actively involved in bisexual community events who subscribed to or recognised alternative looks. Despite the potential for associating alternative looks and looking with bisexuality, bisexual people ultimately remain invisible to other bisexual people outside their communities, and to others in the wider culture (Hayfield, 2013; Hayfield et al., 2013; Huxley et al., 2014).

BOX 4.3 A LACK OF BISEXUAL VISUAL IDENTITIES

While recognisable images of lesbian and gay people exist, there are seemingly no equivalent images of bisexual or pansexual (or asexual, or plurisexual) people. Nonetheless, research has identified various possible ways in which bisexual (and to some extent perhaps pansexual) people may manage their appearance to (try to) convey their sexuality and fit into wider LGBTQ+ spaces (Clarke & Smith, 2015; Daly et al., 2018; Davila, Jabbour, Dyar, & Feinstein, 2019; Hartman, 2013; Hayfield et al., 2013; Holliday, 1999; Rothblum, 2010).

"Borrowing" from lesbian and gay looks

Due to a lack of distinctive bisexual looks, some bisexual and pansexual people have reported that they "borrow" elements of (butch/androgynous) lesbian and (effeminate) gay appearance, particularly when they first come out as bisexual, and often in order to feel they belong within particular spaces (Clarke & Smith, 2015; Clarke & Spence, 2013; Daly et al., 2018; Davila et al., 2019; Hartman, 2013; Hayfield et al., 2013; Rothblum, 2010; Taub, 1999). The notion of the androgynous bisexual is perhaps unsurprising given the early sex researchers' conceptualisations of bisexuality as a mixture of masculinity and femininity (Wolff, 1977; see Chapter 2). However, others have specifically reported wanting to resist conforming to butch looks (Daly et al., 2018).

Looking "somewhere in between"

Bisexual (and perhaps pansexual) women may also carve a space for self-expression by looking "somewhere in between" lesbian and heterosexual. This is often through balancing elements of femininity and masculinity in their appearance (Daly et al., 2018; Hartman, 2013; Hayfield, 2013; Hayfield et al., 2013; Rothblum, 2010). It has been noted that this strategy forces a reliance on binaries of gender and sexuality (Daly et al., 2018; Hayfield et al., 2013). Bisexual (and perhaps pansexual) women have also reported that they change their appearance by adopting aspects of masculine or feminine dress and appearance at particular times, or within particular locations, therefore being highly invested in adapting their appearance according to the situation (Daly et al., 2018; Davila et al., 2019).

Looking a bit alternative

Another possibility is for bisexual people to embrace elements of alternative looks and looking, particularly within bisexual communities and at other bisexual events. This has included Goth and hippy looks, as well as dressing in ways which stand out from the mainstream, such as brightly coloured hair and clothing, piercings, and tattoos (Clarke & Spence, 2013; Daly et al., 2018; Davila et al., 2019; Hayfield, 2013; Hayfield et al., 2013; Holliday, 1999; Huxley et al., 2014).

Being influenced by the gender of their partner

One aspect of bisexual identities which may impact on appearance is the gender of a current partner/partners, which is unlikely to be a factor for lesbians, gay men, or heterosexual people. Some bisexual participants in same-sex/gender relationships have spoken of looking traditionally feminine, and have explicitly avoided subscribing to lesbian looks. In contrast, others in different-sex/gender relationships have sometimes reported adopting butch looks (Daly et al., 2018). Bisexual women in relationships with men have reported feeling pressure to comply with heterosexual appearance norms (and accordingly have adhered to some "traditional" notions of beauty and femininity) (Daly et al., 2018; Taub, 1999). However, other bisexual women in relationships with men have reported adopting short hair and androgynous clothing. They attribute this partly to wanting to express that they are not heterosexual and partly to being unconcerned with men's assessment of their appearance (Taub, 1999). These bisexual women may have found a way to "keep their bisexuality alive" when in monogamous relationships – within which bisexuality is often misrecognised based on partner gender (see Daly et al., 2018). However, some participants have reported that partner gender does not influence their appearance (Taub, 1999).

Feeling invisible

Bisexual and pansexual people lack a distinct visual identity of their own, because their appearance is subsumed within either lesbian and gay looks or gendered heterosexual appearance norms. While bisexual and pansexual people may manage their appearance in ways which interlink with their sexualities, the main possibilities for conveying bisexuality (and perhaps pansexuality) require them to "borrow" elements from a variety of other subcultural looks. The result is that there are no exclusively bisexual looks, and bisexual people are unlikely to be recognisable to others. As a consequence, bisexual (and pansexual) people have reported that they feel invisible as bisexual (Clarke & Smith, 2015; Clarke & Spence, 2013; Clarke & Turner, 2007; Daly et al., 2018; Hayfield et al., 2013; Holliday, 1999; Taub, 1999).

The limitations and complexities of sexuality and appearance norms

While appearance and visual identities have served functions for lesbian and gay people, these are not without considerable limitations and complexities. These types of issues have been little explored in relation to bisexual, pansexual, asexual, and plurisexual identities but may also extend to them.

The dictates of appearance

Dress and appearance may seem to some to be a mandatory requirement, and lesbian and gay people (and perhaps bisexual, pansexual, asexual, and plurisexual people) can feel pressured to adhere to particular looks in particular spaces. Conforming to these looks may mean losing a sense of individuality and a sense of an authentic self beyond their lesbian, gay, or bisexual identity (e.g., Clarke & Spence, 2013; Hutson, 2010). Indeed, bisexual people have sometimes reported that a lack of bisexual look is beneficial in being able to present an authentic self beyond the confines of particular appearance norms (Clarke & Spence, 2013; Hartman, 2013; Hayfield et al., 2013; Rothblum, 2010). Yet those who do not comply with appearance norms within particular LGBTQ+ spaces may struggle to feel that they belong. This arises as a result of others questioning their authenticity as gay or lesbian, treating them as suspicious, subjecting them to disapproving looks and unwanted comments, or even ignoring them and refusing them entry to venues. This can be constraining and frustrating, and indicates that lesbian and gay appearance norms are sometimes as restrictive as the rules of gendered heterosexual society (Clarke & Smith, 2015; Clarke & Spence, 2013; Clarke & Turner, 2007; Daly et al., 2018; Hutson, 2010; Levitt & Hiestand, 2005; Myers et al., 1999; Reddy-Best & Pedersen, 2015). Those who *do* subscribe to particular looks may also face distinctive challenges. Scholars have noted that both butch and femme identities are subject to pathologisation, and have termed this butchphobia (Halberstam, 1998) and femmephobia (Levitt & Hiestand, 2005). This pathologisation arises from lack of conformity to patriarchal gender norms and of being understood as behaving like men (in the case of butch lesbians), or from colluding with the patriarchy and not being seen as "real lesbians" due to the privileging of androgynous and/or masculine looks in lesbian spaces (in the case of femme lesbians) (Levitt & Hiestand, 2005). Further, when heterosexual people "get the message" about lesbian and gay identities based on appearance, visibility can become vulnerability. This can mean that those whose sexualities are most visible to (phobic) others may be more open to societal disapproval, discrimination, hate crimes, and violence (Clarke & Smith, 2015; Daly et al., 2018; Hayfield, 2013; Krakauer & Rose, 2002).

Age and appearance

Lesbians, gay men, and queer people may alter their appearance when they first come out. However, this can be (to some degree) temporary. The expression of sexuality may become less critical as people age and feel more secure within their identities. Accordingly, older people may feel less pressure to comply with appearance norms than younger gay men and lesbians (Barry & Martin, 2016; Clarke & Smith, 2015; Clarke & Spence, 2013; Myers et al., 1999; Reddy-Best & Pedersen, 2015; Taub, 1999).

Diversity and intersecting identities

Our identities are not monolithic; instead we occupy multiple, potentially ever-changing, intersecting, overlapping, but sometimes conflicting, identities. This means that the relationship between our selves, our identities, our social worlds, and our appearance can be particularly complex, and may require ongoing negotiation. For example, traditional notions of masculinity and femininity may have different meanings according to intersections of race and ethnicity (Barry & Martin, 2016; Cole, 2019; Luzzatto & Gvion, 2004). For some lesbians, gay men, bisexual, and pansexual (and asexual, and plurisexual) people of faith and/or Colour, navigating multiple identities may raise various tensions, both as individuals and within collective spaces (Barry & Martin, 2016; Levy & Harr, 2018; Nagel, 2000). Further, it may be that those who occupy biracial/multiracial and bisexual/pansexual identities find that more than one of their identities are invisible to others and that they are at considerable risk of being misread or ignored in multiple ways (e.g., King, 2011, 2013).

Working-class lesbians may be more likely to convey their sexuality through appearance and to engage in butch aesthetics than middle-class lesbians. However, contemporary gay, bisexual, and trans scene spaces are often mainly middle-class. Boundaries may exist between those who can/do or cannot/do not conform to the requirements of these spaces, which can become intimidating, and has left some working-class members feeling marginalised (Taylor, 2007, 2008). There may also be intersections between sexualities and other subcultural identities. Lesbian and bisexual women have been associated with natural looks in similar ways to hippy identities. Goth and punk looks may also be associated with particular sexualities. as well as intersecting with race and ethnicity (Cole, 2000, 2019; Kaiser, 2012; see Box 4.3). The complexity of managing appearance in relation to multiple identities has also been reported to lead to ambivalence and tension (Reddy-Best & Pedersen, 2015; Rosenberg & Sharp, 2018). However, the intersections of identities remain a relatively underexplored area of appearance research.

A changing culture?

Lesbian and gay styles may have been highly functional during the early years of lesbian and gay identities and communities. However, they may hold less currency than they once did, and be less distinctive than they once were (Clarke & Smith, 2015; Clarke & Spence, 2013; Cole, 2000; Hayfield & Wood, 2019; Huxley et al., 2014). Lesbian and gay looks may have diminished in recent years and be less taken up by young people. This could be for a number of reasons. First, homonormalisation – the acceptance and assimilation of (particular types of) lesbian and gay identities into wider heterosexual society – may mean that the importance of sexuality has become downplayed (see Mathers, Sumerau, & Cragun, 2018 for discussion and critique of homonormalisation). Some of the functions that dress and appearance served are therefore sometimes understood as no longer necessary within what is perceived to be a climate of equality (Hayfield & Wood, 2019). Second, aspects of what made lesbian and gay styles distinctive in the past have become incorporated into the mainstream (Clarke & Spence, 2013; Huxley et al., 2014). This can be demonstrated in the metrosexual heterosexual man, who may be highly invested in his appearance in ways more usually associated with heterosexual women and gay men (Clarke & Smith, 2015). Third, from the 1970s onwards there has been some considerable breaking down of binaries, and more fluid understandings of gender and sexuality. In turn, some people resist or subvert traditionally dichotomous ideas and embrace gender fluidity (Barry & Martin, 2016; Cole, 2019). Accordingly, notions of "masculine lesbians" and "feminine gay men" may be becoming (or have already become) outdated (Barry & Martin, 2016; Cole, 2019; Hutson, 2010; Reddy-Best & Pedersen, 2015).

Some images (in particular of butch lesbians and effeminate gay men) have been portrayed somewhat simplistically in one-dimensional or monolithic ways and based mainly on oversimplified stereotypical media representations. Therefore, while they remain recognisable, they are not necessarily a reflection of the nuances within shared spaces (Clarke & Smith, 2015; Clarke & Spence, 2013; Hayfield & Wood, 2019). Research has identified that bisexual people's visual identities may also be nuanced and complex, albeit in somewhat different ways from lesbian and gay visual identities (Clarke & Turner, 2007; Daly et al., 2018; Hayfield, 2013; Taub, 1999). Little is known about trans, asexual, pansexual, or plurisexual identities in relation to sexuality and appearance. In sum, the most dominant theme around bisexual (and this may extend to pansexual, asexual, and plurisexual) appearance is that these groups seemingly have no particular *distinct* visual identities, despite research participants offering narratives of attempting to express their sexuality through their appearance. This may mean that bisexual (and pansexual, asexual, and plurisexual) people are unlikely to be able to convey their sexuality, recognise others, or be recognised by others on the basis of their sexuality. This lack of bisexual (and pansexual, asexual, and plurisexual) looks and looking therefore contributes to the lack of visibility of bisexuality, pansexuality, asexuality, and plurisexualities.

References

Barry, B., & Martin, D. (2016). Gender rebels: Inside the wardrobes of young gay men with subversive style. *Fashion, Style & Popular Culture, 3*(2), 225–250. doi:10.1386/fspc.3.2.225_1

Brennan, S. (2011). Fashion and sexual identity, or why recognition matters. In J. Wolfendale, & J. Kennett (Eds.), *Fashion – Philosophy for everyone: Thinking with style* (pp. 120–134). Chichester: Blackwell. doi:10.1002/9781444345568.ch8

Brennan, S., & Behrensen, M. (2012). Margins within the marginal: Bi-invisibility and intersexual passing. In D. R. Cooley, & K. Harrison (Eds.), *Passing/out: Sexual identity veiled and revealed* (pp. 171–202). Farnham: Ashgate.

Brill, D. (2008). *Goth culture: Gender, sexuality and style.* Oxford: Berg. doi:10.2752/9781847887184

Clarke, V., & Smith, M. (2015). "Not hiding, not shouting, just me": Gay men negotiate their visual identities. *Journal of Homosexuality, 62*(1), 4–32. doi:10.1080/00918369.2014.957119

Clarke, V., & Spence, K. (2013). "I am who I am"? Navigating norms and the importance of authenticity in lesbian and bisexual women's accounts of their appearance practices. *Psychology & Sexuality, 4*(1), 25–33. doi:10.1080/19419899.2013.748240

Clarke, V., & Turner, K. (2007). Clothes maketh the queer? Dress, appearance and the construction of gay, lesbian and bisexual identities. *Feminism and Psychology, 17*(2), 267–276. doi:10.1177/0959353507076561

Cole, S. (2000). *Don we now our gay apparel: Gay men's dress in the twentieth century.* Oxford: Berg. doi:10.2752/9781847888679

Cole, S. (2019). The difference is in the detail: Negotiating black gay male style in the twenty-first century. *Dress, 45*(1), 39–54. doi:10.1080/03612112.2019.1557833

Daly, S., King, N., & Yeadon-Lee, T. (2018). "Femme it up or dress it down": Appearance and bisexual women in monogamous relationships. *Journal of Bisexuality, 18*(3), 257–277. doi:10.1080/15299716.2018.1485071

Davis, F. (1992). *Fashion, culture, and identity.* Chicago: University of Chicago Press. doi:10.7208/chicago/9780226167954.001.0001

Davila, J., Jabbour, J., Dyar, C., & Feinstein, B. A. (2019). Bi+ visibility: Characteristics of those who attempt to make their bisexual+ identity visible and the strategies they use. *Archives of Sexual Behavior, 48*(1), 199–211.

Esterberg, K. G. (1996). "A certain swagger when I walk": Performing lesbian identity. In S. Seidman (Ed.), *Queer theory/sociology* (pp. 259–279). Oxford: Blackwell.

Franklin, A. (2001). Black women and self-presentation: Appearing in (dis)guise. In M. Banim, E. E. Green, & A. Guy (Eds.), *Through the wardrobe: Women's relationships with their clothes* (pp. 137–150). Oxford: Berg.

Frith, H., & Gleeson, K. (2003). Youth, beauty and pride: Privileging young bodies. *Psychology of Women Section Review, 5*(2), 23–27.

Gleeson, K., & Frith, H. (2003). Getting noticed: Using clothing to negotiate visibility. *Psychology of Women Section Review, 5*(2), 7–11.

Goffman, E. (1959/1990). *The presentation of self in everyday life.* London: Penguin.

Goffman, E. (1963). *Behavior in public places: Notes on the social organization of gatherings.* New York: Free Press.

Halberstam, J. (1998). *Female masculinity.* Durham, NC: Duke University Press.

Halim, M. L. D., Gutierrez, B. C., Bryant, D. N., Arredondo, M., & Takesako, K. (2018). Gender is what you look like: Emerging gender identities in young children and preoccupation with appearance. *Self and Identity, 17*(4), 455–466. doi:10.1080/15298868.2017.1412344

Hancock, J. H., Strübel, J., Peirson-Smith, A., & Nishida, K. (2017). Global fashions, appearances, aesthetics, and identities. *Journal of Popular Culture, 50*(6), 1165–1167. doi:10.1111/jpcu.12623

Hartman, J. E. (2013). Creating a bisexual display: Making bisexuality visible. *Journal of Bisexuality, 13*(1), 39–62. doi:10.1080/15299716.2013.755727

Hayfield, N. (2013). "Never judge a book by its cover"? Students' understandings of lesbian, gay, and bisexual appearance. *Psychology & Sexuality, 4*(1), 16–24. doi:10.1080/19419899.2013.748261

Hayfield, N., Clarke, V., Halliwell, E., & Malson, H. (2013). Visible lesbians and invisible bisexuals: Appearance and visual identities among bisexual women. *Women's Studies International Forum, 40*(1), 172–182. doi:10.1016/j.wsif.2013.07.015

Hayfield, N., & Wood, M. (2019). Looking heteronormatively good! Combining story completion tasks with Bitstrips to explore understandings of sexuality and appearance. *Qualitative Research in Psychology, 16*(1), 115–135. doi:10.1080/14780887.2018.1536390

Hethorn, J., & Kaiser, S. (1998). Youth style: Articulating cultural anxiety. *Visual Studies, 14*(1), 109–125. doi:10.1080/14725869908583805

Holliday, R. (1999). The comfort of identity. *Sexualities, 2*(4), 475–491. doi:10.1177/136346099002004007

Hollingworth, S., & Williams, K. (2009). Constructions of the working-class "other" among urban, white, middle-class youth: "Chavs", subculture and the valuing of education. *Journal of Youth Studies, 12*(5), 467–482. doi:10.1080/13676260903081673

Hutson, D. J. (2010). Standing out/fitting in: Identity, appearance, and authenticity in gay and lesbian communities. *Symbolic Interaction, 33*(2), 213–233. doi:10.1525/si.2010.33.2.213

Huxley, C., Clarke, V., & Halliwell, E. (2014). Resisting and conforming to the "lesbian look": The importance of appearance norms for lesbian and bisexual women. *Journal of Community & Applied Social Psychology, 24*(3), 205–219. doi:10.1002/casp.2161

Jankowski, G. S., Diedrichs, P. C., Williamson, H., Christopher, G., & Harcourt, D. (2016). Looking age-appropriate while growing old gracefully: A qualitative study of ageing and body image among older adults. *Journal of Health Psychology, 21*(4), 550–561. doi:10.1177/1359105314531468

Kaiser, S. B. (1998). *The social psychology of clothing: Symbolic appearances in context* (2nd ed.). New York: Macmillan.

Kaiser, S. B. (2012). *Fashion and cultural studies*. London: Bloomsbury Academic.

King, A. R. (2011). Are we coming of age? A critique of Collins's proposed model of biracial–bisexual identity development. *Journal of Bisexuality, 11*(1), 98–120. doi:10.1080/15299716.2011.545314

King, A. R. (2013). Mixed messages: How primary agents of socialization influence adolescent females who identify as multiracial–bisexual. *Journal of LGBT Youth, 10*(4), 308–327. doi:10.1080/19361653.2013.825198

Krakauer, I. D., & Rose, S. M. (2002). The impact of group membership on lesbians' physical appearance. *Journal of Lesbian Studies, 6*(1), 31–43. doi:10.1300/J155v06n01_04

Levitt, H. M., & Hiestand, K. R. (2005). Gender within lesbian sexuality: Butch and femme perspectives. *Journal of Constructivist Psychology, 18*(1), 39–51. doi:10.1080/10720530590523062

Levy, D. L., & Harr, J. (2018). "I never felt like there was a place for me:" Experiences of bisexual and pansexual individuals with a Christian upbringing. *Journal of Bisexuality, 18*(2), 186–205. doi:10.1080/15299716.2018.1431169

Lewis, V. D. (2010). Hip-hop fashion. In V. Steele (Ed.), *The Berg companion to fashion* (pp. 413–417). Oxford: Bloomsbury Academic.

Luzzatto, D., & Gvion, L. (2004). Feminine but not femme. *Journal of Homosexuality*, *48*(1), 43–77. doi:10.1300/J082v48n01_03

Maliepaard, E. (2018). Spaces with a bisexual appearance: Re-conceptualizing bisexual space (s) through a study of bisexual practices in the Netherlands. *Social & Cultural Geography*, 1–19. doi:10.1080/14649365.2018.1454979

Mathers, L. A., Sumerau, J. E., & Cragun, R. T. (2018). The limits of homonormativity: Constructions of bisexual and transgender people in the post-gay era. *Sociological Perspectives*, *61*(6), 934–952. doi:10.1177/0731121417753370

Myers, A., Taub, J., Morris, J. F., & Rothblum, E. D. (1999). Beauty mandates and the appearance obsession: Are lesbian and bisexual women better off? *Journal of Lesbian Studies*, *3*(4), 15–26. doi:10.1300/J155v03n04_03

Nagel, J. (2000). Ethnicity and sexuality. *Annual Review of Sociology*, *26*(1), 107–133. doi:10.1146/annurev.soc.26.1.107

Peel, E. (2005). Effeminate 'fudge nudgers' and tomboyish 'lettuce lickers': Language and the construction of sexualities in diversity training. *Psychology of Women Section Review*, *7*(2), 22–34.

Polhemus, T. (1996). *Style surfing: What to wear in the 3rd millennium*. London: Thames & Hudson.

Reddy-Best, K. L., & Pedersen, E. L. (2015). The relationship of gender expression, sexual identity, distress, appearance, and clothing choices for queer women. *International Journal of Fashion Design, Technology and Education*, *8*(1), 54–65. doi:10.1080/17543266.2014.958576

Rosenberg, S., & Sharp, M. (2018). Documenting queer(ed) punk histories: Instagram, archives and ephemerality. *Queer Studies in Media & Popular Culture*, *3*(2), 159–174. doi:10.1386/qsmpc.3.2.159_1

Rothblum, E. D. (1994). Lesbians and physical appearance: Which model applies? In B. Greene, & G. M. Herek (Eds.), *Lesbian and gay psychology: Theory, research, and clinical applications* (pp. 84–97). Thousand Oaks: Sage. doi:10.4135/9781483326757.n5

Rothblum, E. D. (2010). The complexity of butch and femme among sexual minority women in the 21st century. *Psychology of Sexualities Review*, *1*(1), 29–42.

Taub, J. (1999). Bisexual women and beauty norms: A qualitative examination. *Journal of Lesbian Studies*, *3*(4), 27–36. doi:10.1300/J155v03n04_04

Taylor, Y. (2007). "If your face doesn't fit … ": The misrecognition of working-class lesbians in scene space. *Leisure Studies*, *26*(2), 161–178. doi:10.1080/02614360600661211

Taylor, Y. (2008). "That's not really my scene": Working-class lesbians in (and out of) place. *Sexualities*, *11*(5), 523–546. doi:10.1177/1363460708094266

Tierney, T. (2017). Appropriation, articulation and authentication in acid house: The evolution of women's fashion throughout the early years (1987–1988) of the acid house culture. *Fashion, Style & Popular Culture*, *4*(2), 179–196. doi:10.1386/fspc.4.2.179_1

Todd, E. R., & Funder, D. C. (2016). Personality. In D. E. Matsumoto, H. C. Hwang, & M. G. Frank (Eds.), *APA handbook of nonverbal communication* (pp. 163–185). Washington, DC: American Psychological Association. doi:10.1037/14669-007

Twigg, J. (2007). Clothing, age and the body: A critical review. *Ageing & Society*, *27*(2), 285–305. doi:10.1017/S0144686X06005794

van Elferen, I., & Weinstock, J. A. (2016). *Goth music: From sound to subculture*. London: Routledge. doi:10.4324/9781315867199

Welters, L. (2008). The natural look: American style in the 1970s. *Fashion Theory*, *12*(4), 489–510. doi:10.2752/175174108X346959

Widdicombe, S., & Wooffitt, R. (1995). *The language of youth subcultures: Social identity in action*. Hemel Hempstead: Harvester Wheatsheaf.

Wolff, C. (1977). *Bisexuality: A study*. London: Quartet Books.

Ylänne, D. V. (Ed.). (2012). *Representing ageing*. Basingstoke: Palgrave Macmillan. doi:10.1057/9781137009340

5

THE ERASURE AND EXCLUSION OF BISEXUAL, PANSEXUAL, ASEXUAL, AND PLURISEXUAL PEOPLE WITHIN EDUCATION, EMPLOYMENT, AND MAINSTREAM MASS MEDIA

The focus in this chapter is on individual and cultural invisibility through an exploration of how bisexual, pansexual, asexual, and plurisexual identities are invisible within three specific contexts – education, the workplace, and the mainstream mass media – and on how if these identities *are* made visible they are often invalidated or erased. These foci enable a consideration of invisibility within important organisational contexts which most people will encounter during their lives (e.g., in schools and workplaces), and an exploration of wider cultural representations of bisexual, pansexual, asexual, and plurisexual people within mass media. The focus on these three areas is also partially pragmatic in relation to the limited literature which exists on bisexual, pansexual, asexual, and plurisexual in/visibility. The chapter also reports analysis based on the existing literature of how invisibility and invalidation impact on people's experiences of school, work, and media consumption. The small body of extant research in these areas focuses mainly on bisexuality, with some recent research specifically on pansexuality and asexuality. Occasionally additional plurisexual identities are included, but often these are subsumed within other identities. The identities specifically mentioned in these publications are listed in the text; those not included are listed in parentheses, to acknowledge them and indicate that the arguments being made could potentially be extended to include them. However, there are likely to be both similarities and differences in the experiences of these groups of people, and further research is needed to develop a clearer understanding of their in/visibility and in/validation.

The invisibility and invalidation of bisexual, pansexual, asexual, and plurisexual identities in schools

Sexuality and sex and relationship education

The teaching of sex and relationship education in schools has historically been fraught with tension, especially in relation to the inclusion of LGBTQ+ topics (Gegenfurtner & Gebhardt, 2017; Greenland & Nunney, 2008). In the UK this is partly attributable to Section 28, which was introduced by the Conservative government in 1988. This now notorious legislation stated that local authorities should not "intentionally promote homosexuality" within schools. Section 28 was controversial. It caused confusion and uncertainty about what constituted the "intentional promotion of homosexuality" and created a climate of fear, including for teachers who consequently often avoided mentioning same-sex/gender sexualities in their lessons at all (Epstein, 2000; Greenland & Nunney, 2008; Walker & Bates, 2016). Section 28 contributed to an oppressive climate where LGBTQ+ bullying in schools persisted, and the needs of LGBTQ+ students were silenced or ignored (Epstein, 2000; Greenland & Nunney, 2008).

The Labour government repealed Section 28 in 2003, following much political campaigning by Stonewall and LGBTQ+ people. Nonetheless, heterosexuality is often implicitly and explicitly taught as the only valid option and as what should be embraced – regardless of students' diverse sexualities. Therefore, schools are often heteronormative, heterocentric, and hostile environments for young LGBTQ+ people – both within and outside the UK (Barker, 2007; Elia, 2010; Francis, 2017; McAllum, 2018). It has been reported that young people are aware of negative societal stereotypes about their identities and that these are sometimes reinforced within schools by their peers and teachers. This environment has meant that young LGBTQ+ people have modified their behaviours (e.g., how they walk and talk) to conceal their sexuality. Prejudice, discrimination, and homophobia persist, and these manifest in various forms of verbal harassment – including the derogatory use of the phrase "that's so gay" – and physical bullying. Such incidents significantly impact on young LGBTQ+ people's well-being, attendance, and academic achievements. However, prejudice and discrimination may go unreported or unchallenged by peers or staff, who have sometimes been reported to be unsupportive of LGBTQ+ youth (Barker, 2007; Elia, 2010; Gegenfurtner & Gebhardt, 2017; Greenland & Nunney, 2008; McAllum, 2018; Rivers, 2004; Walker & Bates, 2016). This type of school environment can result in a range of negative outcomes for young LGBTQ+ people, including fears of being bullied and harassed, feeling humiliated, helpless, vulnerable, isolated, excluded, and as though they have few friends, and no one to talk to (e.g., Rivers, 2004; Rivers, Gonzalez, Nodin, Peel, & Tyler, 2018). LGBTQ+ youth who are bullied can experience low self-esteem and depression and may self-harm or consider suicide (see Rivers, 2018). Further, LGBTQ+ people's experiences of school may also have long-lasting implications into adulthood (Rivers, 2004, 2011).

Invisibility within school environments, policies, curricula, and extracurricular activities

The word bisexuality is "rarely if ever uttered" within the classroom (Elia, 2010, p. 457). There is minimal information about the experiences and needs of bisexual and pansexual (and asexual and plurisexual) students (Elia, 2010; Francis, 2017; Jones & Hillier, 2014; Kennedy & Fisher, 2010; McAllum, 2018). Bisexuality (and pansexuality, asexuality, and plurisexual identities) are often only vaguely referred to in school policies, curricula, or teaching guidelines (Elia, 2010; McAllum, 2014, 2018). When attraction to more than one gender *is* mentioned, it is rarely named. Instead, those who are bisexual or pansexual (or asexual or plurisexual) are either subsumed within LGBTQ+ identities – despite the fact their experiences are likely to differ from each other's – or become entirely overlooked (Elia, 2010; Francis, 2017; Jones & Hillier, 2014; Kennedy & Fisher, 2010; McAllum, 2014, 2018). The invisibility of bisexuality and pansexuality (and asexuality and plurisexual identities) has also been reported to extend to extracurricular activities, including gay–straight alliances (Elia, 2010; Kennedy & Fisher, 2010; Lapointe, 2017). The impact of the lack of meaningful inclusion of diverse sexualities within school environments has been little researched (Francis, 2017; Jones & Hillier, 2014; Kennedy & Fisher, 2010; Lapointe, 2017; McAllum, 2014, 2018). What findings do exist indicate that invisibility and lack of inclusion perpetuate the notions that bisexual and pansexual (and asexual and plurisexual) identities are neither valid nor legitimate. What is taught in the classroom often reinforces binary and monosexist notions of gender and sexuality – and silences or misrepresents bisexuality and pansexuality (and asexuality and plurisexuality) (Elia, 2010; Francis, 2017; Lapointe, 2017; McAllum, 2014, 2018).

Bisexual, pansexual, asexual, and plurisexual students' experiences of school

Some researchers and organisations have conducted school climate studies with students who are lesbian, gay, bisexual, pansexual, or asexual, or who identify with plurisexualities (for an example, see Box 5.1). These reports have sometimes included bisexuality in their publication titles, or detailed in their reports how many students identify with particular sexualities. However, the remainder of the document often omits any focused consideration of specific identities. Therefore, young bisexual, pansexual, asexual, and plurisexual people may seem to be included but are effectively excluded and their experiences erased (Jones & Hillier, 2014; McAllum, 2018). The Gay, Lesbian, and Straight Education Network (GLSEN) in the US has done considerable work to support young LGBTQ+ people. Its surveys have meaningfully included large numbers of participants and made efforts to recruit diverse sexualities (see Box 5.1). However, as Elia (2010) highlights, the organisation's name does not portray this inclusion of asexual, bisexual, pansexual, questioning, and trans students (Elia, 2010; McAllum, 2018). This results in a scenario where particular sexualities are seemingly *excluded* even when they are *included*.

BOX 5.1 GAY, LESBIAN, AND STRAIGHT EDUCATION NET-WORK (GLSEN)

Despite the organisation's name including no mention of bisexual, pansexual, asexual, or plurisexual identities, GLSEN's research has included diverse sexualities. In its 2015 online survey of over 10,000 young LGBTQ+ people, recruitment was online via social media and via a range of relevant groups and organisations (rather than directly through schools). While 22.9% were bisexual, 16.1% were pansexual (indicating the increased prevalence of these identities among young people; see also Lapointe, 2017). The survey asked participants broad quantitative questions about topics such as safety, harassment, assault, and discrimination within schools. Bisexual students reported that they felt safer, and had experienced less victimisation in school, than gay, lesbian, or pansexual students. While this might be interpreted as a result of their being less "out" than other sexuality groups, and therefore less visible, bisexual students also reported higher levels of sexual harassment. They were also less likely than gay and lesbian students to report incidents to staff. Additionally, compared with lesbian and gay pupils, bisexual students had lower scores on self-esteem and sense of belonging, but higher scores on depression. Pansexual students and those with other sexual identities (e.g., asexual, questioning) scored even more poorly.

GLSEN highlights the need for bisexual identities to be named, taught about, and discussed within schools (see also Jones & Hillier, 2014; Kennedy & Fisher, 2010), and notes the importance of additional research to fully understand the experiences of students with diverse sexualities (Kosciw, Greytak, Giga, Villenas, & Danischewski, 2016). GLSEN offers various resources on bisexuality in schools. These include videos with bisexual students who discuss their definitions of bisexuality and report how bisexuality has been overlooked in school curricula (www.glsen.org/supporting-bisexual-students).

Few research studies have specifically explored bisexual, pansexual, asexual, and plurisexual pupils' experiences of school. Those that have indicate that the lack of inclusion or affirmation of their sexualities results in their feeling that their identities are ignored and that they are excluded (Barker, 2007; Hillier & Mitchell, 2008; Lapointe, 2017; McAllum, 2014, 2018; Rothblum, Heimann, & Carpenter, 2019). In a US study with asexual students, some felt that their identity was an advantage because they were not distracted from their studies by thinking about physical attraction to others. However, other participants reported that anxiety about being different distracted them from their studies, or that they felt lonely and left out when their peers were focused on dating (Rothblum et al., 2019). Peers and teachers have reportedly responded to bisexuality and pansexuality negatively, with some invalidating these sexualities as non-existent, as a temporary stage, as women purely seeking the attention of heterosexual men, or as promiscuous, hypersexual, and linked to sexual disease (Francis, 2017; Lapointe, 2017; McAllum, 2014; see Chapter 3). In a Canadian study, pansexual students reported that peers and teachers did not understand pansexuality, or were confused by its disruption of sex/gender binaries. Therefore, some students took responsibility for educating others about their sexuality (Lapointe, 2017).

It is possible that those with bisexual (and pansexual, asexual, and plurisexual) identities, like lesbian and gay people, are open to bullying and harassment (Elia, 2010). US researchers recruited middle-school and high-school pupils aged 14–19 to explore victimisation in their homes, schools, and wider lives. Bisexual and pansexual participants reported higher rates of some forms of emotional and physical victimisation than gay participants (Sterzing et al., 2019). In other studies, bisexual students have reported being bullied and discriminated against by peers, which in some instances they did not feel able to report to teachers (Francis, 2017; McAllum, 2014, 2018).

In a South African study, researchers conducted interviews and classroom observations with 33 (mainly heterosexual) teachers and interviews with three young bisexual men and two young bisexual women (all aged 16–19 years). The authors concluded that most teachers understood bisexuality in ways which linked with common cultural understandings (see Chapter 3), including as confused, in a temporary transitionary phase, attention-seeking, and hypersexual. The students reported experiences of biphobia which also mirrored these cultural understandings but wanted their bisexuality to be recognised and respected. However, there were some more positive accounts where a few teachers demonstrated some openness to learning about lesbian, gay, and bisexual identities (Francis, 2017).

In Aotearoa New Zealand-based research, 36 bisexual women (aged 16–24) were asked about their experiences of secondary school. Data collection was via focus groups, interviews, and journals. Students reported that their schools had been heteronormative environments. One young bisexual woman reported that she was ignored, and excluded from female changing rooms, as a result of her bisexuality. Another told of how one teacher distanced themselves from her, made discriminatory remarks about sexually diverse identities, and offered her less academic support than they had before she had come out as bisexual (McAllum, 2018). These types of experiences may extend to pansexual, asexual, and plurisexual students and demonstrate that further work is needed to ensure that teachers are aware of diverse identities and that schools are safe and inclusive environments for students.

Schools are arguably a microcosm of the wider societal context of invisibility of and hostility towards bisexuality (and pansexuality, asexuality, and plurisexuality) (Elia, 2010). Bisexual (and pansexual, asexual, and plurisexual) identities may also be invisible or invalidated in higher education, including on university campuses, and in curriculum and course content (Barker, 2007; Formby, 2017). This "systematic erasure" of bisexuality has been described as "a form of violence and neglect" (Elia, 2010, p. 458). The meaningful inclusion of diverse genders and sexualities is an essential requirement if schools and universities are to be safe and supportive environments that reflect and respect young people's identities (Elia, 2010; Lapointe, 2017). The United Nations Educational, Scientific, and Cultural Organization (UNESCO) has issued policies and guidance on how to tackle homophobic bullying in schools. UNESCO members have recognised that bisexuality has been overlooked. They intend to discuss bisexuality in their statements (see Jones & Hillier, 2014). Whether the intention is also to include pansexuality, asexuality, and plurisexual identities is not known.

The invisibility of bisexual, pansexual, asexual, and plurisexual identities within the workplace

Bisexual, pansexual, asexual, and plurisexual people and their identities are often invisible or invalidated within workplace policies and workplace culture (Chamberlain, 2009/2012; Popova, 2018; See & Hunt, 2011). However, studies which have explored sexuality in the workplace have most commonly focused on lesbian and gay identities, or have subsumed bisexual (and pansexual, asexual, and plurisexual) identities within broader LGBTQ+ research (Köllen, 2013; Popova, 2018). In one study, bisexual participants' results were analysed separately, but the word bisexual was excluded from the title and abstract of the report (Carpenter, 2008). Therefore, such research is hard to locate and easily overlooked. Overall, there is minimal research or knowledge specifically about bisexuality, pansexuality, asexuality, and plurisexual identities in the workplace (Köllen, 2013; Popova, 2018; Rothblum et al., 2019).

Invisibility within workplace policies and LGBTQ+ staff networks

Historically, workplace policies and practices have privileged heterosexual employees, especially those who conform to traditional notions of marriage and children. Therefore, those who are single, childfree, and/or LGBTQ+ have been marginalised and othered which has impacted on their experiences of the workplace and on their careers (Compton & Dougherty, 2017; Dixon & Dougherty, 2014; Harding & Peel, 2007; Williams & Giuffre, 2011). It is only relatively recently that lesbian and gay people have been offered the potential protection and benefits of being included in workplace policies (Compton & Dougherty, 2017; Harding & Peel, 2007). However, bisexual and pansexual (and asexual and plurisexual) people often remain invisible within policies, procedures, and other resources (Chamberlain, 2009/2012; Green, Payne, & Green, 2011; Popova, 2018; See & Hunt, 2011). Equality and diversity policies commonly subsume bisexuality, and other diverse sexualities, under the wider LGBTQ+ umbrella (Green et al., 2011). Discrimination on the basis of sexuality may be a matter of misconduct, but bisexuality and other identities are unlikely to be explicitly mentioned, and hence are not meaningfully included (Köllen, 2013).

Bisexual (and pansexual, asexual, and plurisexual) people may also feel excluded because equal rights are frequently framed around same-sex/gender relationships as equal to different-sex/gender relationships – for example, in relation to company benefits such as health insurance, pensions, and parental and compassionate leave (Köllen, 2013). Equality may also relate to feeling able to be open about same-sex/gender partners and in a position to bring them to workplace social events (Popova, 2018). Additionally, many diversity-related marketing activities draw on images of same-sex/gender couples (Köllen, 2013). However, this focus on same-sex/gender relationships may not meet the needs of bisexual (or pansexual, asexual, or plurisexual) people, especially those in different-sex/gender relationships, who may be especially invisible (Köllen, 2013; Popova, 2018). It is therefore unsurprising that bisexual (and pansexual, asexual, and plurisexual) people are sometimes under the impression that equality and diversity policies and procedures do not apply to them. They have reported feeling silenced by this exclusion (Chamberlain, 2009/2012; Compton & Dougherty, 2017). The exclusion of diverse sexualities is also important because workplace policies "reflect and regulate sexual norms for all employees" and therefore inform organisational norms and workplace cultures (Compton & Dougherty, 2017, p. 877).

Employees who are involved with LGBTQ+ networks and communities, including staff networks, are more likely to feel able to be out and open about their sexuality in their lives than those who are not (Green et al., 2011). However, bisexual (and pansexual, asexual, and plurisexual) people have been reported to be somewhat invisible within these networks, which are often comprised of mainly gay men, fewer lesbian women, and even fewer bisexual members (Köllen, 2013). There has been little focus on pansexual, asexual, and plurisexual people and their involvement in LGBTQ+ groups. Those in different-sex/gender relationships have reported that they are seen as allies of LGBTQ+ staff networks, rather than as fully fledged members (Green et al., 2011). Overall, bisexual and pansexual (and asexual and plurisexual) people may feel that they do not belong within employee networks (Chamberlain, 2009/2012; Green et al., 2011; See & Hunt, 2011).

Bisexual, pansexual, asexual, and plurisexual people's experiences in the workplace

There are some studies of bisexual people's experiences in the workplace, but fewer which include pansexual, asexual, or plurisexual identities. Bisexual women in the Netherlands reported higher levels of personal and work-related bullying than heterosexual women. They were also more likely to feel that their opinions were ignored, and reported that they did not have equal promotion opportunities. Both bisexual men and women had higher levels of burnout than their heterosexual counterparts (Kuyper, 2015). In Australia, bisexual women were more likely to report that they had experienced distressing workplace harassment, and were less satisfied with their work and careers, than heterosexual women (Carpenter, 2008). According to British employee-monitoring data, bisexual staff also have some of the lowest staff satisfaction rates (See & Hunt, 2011; Box 5.2).

BOX 5.2 STONEWALL REPORT ON BISEXUALITY IN THE WORKPLACE

The British LGBT charity Stonewall has published results of research specifically exploring bisexuality in the workplace (Chamberlain, 2009/2012). This identified various issues which mirrored those identified in academic studies. These included a lack of support within LGB staff networks or employers' equality and diversity policies and a lack of bisexual-specific visibility. Overall, bisexual people felt invisible in the workplace. There was also reported to be little awareness of or accurate knowledge about bisexuality, possibly arising from this invisibility. This impacted on bisexual people's feelings, expectations, and experiences of coming out. Bisexual participants reported that colleagues held discriminatory and prejudiced views based on negative stereotypes and binary understandings. The report listed recommendations for how organisations could support and engage bisexual employees. These included staff networks and company policies meaningfully including bisexual people (regardless of the gender of their current partner/s) and ensuring that bisexual people were supported with career development opportunities. The authors recommended building awareness about bisexuality in the workplace.

In Canadian research, even though bisexual people were more likely to report that they were very satisfied with their jobs than their heterosexual, lesbian, or gay colleagues, bisexual women more commonly reported high job stress. Further, unmarried bisexual women were less likely to report job satisfaction compared with unmarried heterosexual women (Leppel, 2014). In Switzerland, bisexual men and women perceived less discrimination than lesbian or gay people, but lesbian and bisexual women reported more verbal stigmatisation than gay or bisexual men (Lloren & Parini, 2017). In a recent UK survey, one-fifth of bisexual men and women reported having been sexually assaulted at work. One bisexual woman reported that her manager had witnessed her being sexually assaulted, but had dismissed her colleague's behaviour on the basis of her bisexuality (TUC, 2019).

In relation to asexuality, some US asexual people reported that their identity was not an issue in the workplace. However, one participant spoke of colleagues responding to them coming out as asexual with some confusion. Others spoke of uncertainty around whether their friendliness might be perceived as flirting, or reported that they were expected to work extra hours due to their (being viewed as) not having a family. Another explicitly linked the lack of discussion of sexualities in the workplace to their asexuality being invisible (Rothblum et al., 2019).

Trans people also experience prejudice, discrimination, and harassment from colleagues, and face barriers in their career progression (Levitt & Ippolito, 2014; Ruggs, Martinez, Hebl, & Law, 2015). However, little is known about trans people's workplace experiences, particularly for those who are trans *and* bisexual, pansexual, asexual, or plurisexual. Those who occupy multiple marginalised identities in relation to race and ethnicity, disabilities, age, and so on may have particularly complex experiences. Yet most discrimination research focuses on one aspect of diversity – bearing in mind that some identities may be more salient than others (see below) – with little focus on intersectionality or the impact of multiple marginalisations (D'Allaird, 2016). More broadly, researchers have highlighted that there may be complexities in occupying and managing invisible and stigmatised identities at work (Clair, Beatty, & MacLean, 2005). The overall lack of visibility in the workplace may result in bisexual, pansexual, asexual, and plurisexual individuals thinking that they are the only ones. Consequently, they may feel unable to be out and open, which in turn perpetuates the invisibility of diverse sexualities (Green et al., 2011; Popova, 2018; See & Hunt, 2011).

(Not) coming out in the workplace

Stonewall has reported that 6% of lesbians, 8% of gay men, and 55% of bisexual people are *not* out in British workplaces (See & Hunt, 2011). In the Pew Research Center (2013) *Survey of LGBT Americans*, 50% of lesbians, 48% of gay men, but only 11% of bisexual people reported that most or all of their close colleagues knew about their sexuality. To date, there are seemingly no figures on how out pansexual, asexual, and plurisexual people are at work. It is important to acknowledge the existence of the wider "coming-out imperative" within Western cultures. This disclosure imperative celebrates those who come out as empowered and as good role models, while those who do not come out may become positioned as dishonest and cowardly (McLean, 2007; Rasmussen, 2004). This can result in additional pressures for bisexual (and pansexual, asexual, and plurisexual) people, who may feel guilty about not coming out or for passing as heterosexual, gay, or lesbian (McLean, 2007). The term bisexual self-erasure has been used to refer to how bisexual people may in effect perpetuate their own invisibility by not being out (see Magrath, Cleland, & Anderson, 2017; See & Hunt, 2011). However, there is a risk of blaming those with diverse sexualities for their own invisibility without considering the nuances and complexities of coming out (Green et al., 2011; Magrath et al., 2017; See & Hunt, 2011).

For those with monosexual identities, coming-out strategies can include displaying photographs of their partner, or referring to their partner's gender in conversation. However, partner gender does not reliably indicate the identities of bisexual, pansexual, asexual, and plurisexual people, especially when these identities are rarely even considered a possibility. Instead, explicit statements about identity may be the only viable strategy to disclose sexuality

(Chamberlain, 2009/2012; Compton & Dougherty, 2017; Green et al., 2011; Popova, 2018; See & Hunt, 2011). Sexuality is considered a private matter, whereas the workplace is a public domain, so explicit statements about sexuality may be seen as inappropriate. Accordingly, some bisexual employees have reported concerns that others will think that they are propositioning them, or making an issue of their sexuality, if they come out at work (Popova, 2018).

The requirement to be direct in coming out can mean that those who are ambivalent about the term bisexuality, or identity labels more broadly, may choose not to explicitly name their identities to others. In the US, 53% of bisexual people (compared with 21% of lesbian women and 25% of gay men) consider that their sexuality is "not too or not at all important to their overall identity" (Pew Research Center, 2013, p. 76). The extent to which people feel affiliated with identity labels, or how important their identity is to them, might conceivably contribute to how out bisexual, pansexual, asexual, and plurisexual people are (Magrath et al., 2017; See & Hunt, 2011).

There may be other important reasons why bisexual people are not out and open in the workplace, including fear of negative attention and biphobia (Chamberlain, 2009/2012; See & Hunt, 2011). Those with diverse sexualities may find it particularly challenging to be out to managers and colleagues. Some have reported that senior staff and co-workers have responded to their sexualities with unfriendliness, discomfort, phobic responses, and aggressiveness (Köllen, 2013; Popova, 2018). Bisexual and pansexual (and asexual and plurisexual) people are also likely to experience double discrimination (e.g., both from lesbian and gay people and from heterosexual people) (Green et al., 2011; Köllen, 2013), or multiple discrimination (on the basis of other aspects of their identity) (see Chapter 3). There may also be work-specific sexuality stereotypes. These include that bisexual people are indecisive, disorganised, less reliable, and less able to complete their work as effectively as colleagues (Green et al., 2011; See & Hunt, 2011). Young people who identify with pansexual and plurisexual identities may be marginalised in ways which reflect intergenerational conflict. Those who are millennials (i.e., born between 1980 and 2000) may be perceived through the lens of media portrayals, and therefore as demanding, lazy, uncommitted, disloyal, and unappreciative of their employer's investment in their training (Kehoe, 2018). Biphobia and panphobia (like homophobia) may mean that bisexual, pansexual, asexual, and plurisexual people (similarly to lesbian and gay people) self-silence to self-protect. Silencing is oppressive and reflects the ongoing regulation of sexual identities in the workplace, despite wider developments in recognising some diverse sexualities (Compton & Dougherty, 2017).

People may make daily decisions about whether, how, and to what extent to come out to colleagues (Connell, 2012); hence there are degrees of how out people are. Those with invisible and stigmatised social identities may be out to varying degrees, or only to particular people (Clair et al., 2005; Köllen, 2013). Bisexual, pansexual, asexual, and plurisexual people may find themselves being concerned that others might out them, and may continually assess how their openness has impacted on relationships with co-workers (Leppel, 2014; Popova, 2018). How open those with invisible identities are may also be influenced by personal characteristics (Clair et al., 2005; Köllen, 2013). Those who are dissatisfied with the workplace, and with their personal life circumstances, may be more likely to conceal their bisexual and pansexual (and asexual and plurisexual) identities (Green et al., 2011). Passing as heterosexual – or as lesbian or gay – may impact negatively on work performance, and leave bisexual, pansexual, and plurisexual people feeling isolated and as though they lack authenticity or legitimacy (Clair et al., 2005; Köllen, 2013). Those who are asexual may face similar challenges when passing as allosexual, or concealing aspects of themselves and their lives. Additionally, those who pass as lesbian or gay may encounter workplace discrimination in similar ways to lesbian and gay people (Köllen, 2013).

Further, coming out as lesbian, gay, or bisexual (or pansexual, asexual, or plurisexual) is not a singular event but an ongoing series of events (Connell, 2012; Köllen, 2013; Popova, 2018). This is particularly relevant during organisational restructuring when employees start working with new teams (Köllen, 2013; Popova, 2018). The requirement to come out on multiple occasions can be especially salient for bisexual and plurisexual employees. They may also have to repeatedly come out to the same people, due to notions that their sexualities are temporary, or that their identities cease to exist when they are in long-term relationships (Bisexual Issues Committee, 2018; Popova, 2018). Among the most challenging experiences reported by bisexual and plurisexual people working within psychology professions was their sexuality being invisible or ignored, especially if they had a partner of a different sex/gender (Bisexual Issues Committee, 2018). Others may also assume that bisexual and pansexual (and plurisexual) people are in consensually non-monogamous/polyamorous relationships, which are often misunderstood to be akin to promiscuity and cheating and therefore viewed negatively (Green et al., 2011). Consequently, those who are, or are assumed to be, in multiple relationships are likely to experience additional discrimination in the workplace (Tweedy, 2010). In sum, it may feel safer for bisexual, pansexual, asexual, and plurisexual people to remain invisible rather than disclosing their sexuality within a potentially hostile climate. However, feeling unable to be out has been linked with feeling a lack of authenticity, acknowledgement, or representation.

People of diverse sexualities feeling able to be out and open in the workplace should matter to organisations (see Popova, 2018; See & Hunt, 2011). As a result of exclusionary workplace climates, bisexual and pansexual (and asexual and plurisexual) people may feel overlooked and alienated at work (Chamberlain, 2009/2012; Köllen, 2013; Popova, 2018). To be visible and recognised in the workplace is important for people's sense of authenticity and belonging (Buchanan & Settles, 2019). Invisibility can result in a sense of inauthenticity and feelings of loneliness and isolation (Popova, 2018; see also Buchanan & Settles, 2019; Clair et al., 2005). The implementation of workplace equality and diversity policies is partly based on beliefs that effective diversity management brings positive social and economic effects (Köllen, 2013). Being out at work is often understood to be personally and professionally beneficial for LGBTQ+ people and the organisations they work for (see Bowen & Blackmon, 2003; Lloren & Parini, 2017). There have been links between employees being out and increased productivity, overall happiness, and satisfaction (see Bowen & Blackmon, 2003; Köllen, 2013; Popova, 2018; See & Hunt, 2011). Research has also identified that lesbian, gay, and bisexual employees feel less isolated from teams, projects, and social events, and have lower rates of harassment, in companies where LGBTQ+-supportive policies are implemented (Lloren & Parini, 2017).

Overall, a multitude of factors means that bisexuality, pansexuality, asexuality, and plurisexualities can effectively become unspeakable in the workplace. These factors perpetuate the erasure and invisibility of bisexual (and pansexual, asexual, and plurisexual) people (Popova, 2018). Recommendations for increasing inclusivity in the workplace understandably include advising people to be out about their sexuality and to serve as mentors or role models for others (Chamberlain, 2009/2012; Green et al., 2011). However, the responsibility for overcoming invisibility and discrimination does not *only* lie with individuals. Instead, organisations and other employees have a part to play (for a similar discussion regarding trans discrimination, see Ruggs et al., 2015). Strategies can include using inclusive language, openly talking about diverse sexualities, challenging biphobia, and naming specific sexualities on intranet sites, in internal communications, and within company publications. On the whole, the more inclusive of diverse sexualities the working environment is, the more likely people are to feel included and validated (Bisexual Issues Committee, 2018; Green et al., 2011; Köllen, 2013; also see Harding & Peel, 2007).

Bisexuality, pansexuality, asexuality, and plurisexuality in the media

Bisexuality is notably invisible – and when visible, is often invalidated – within various mainstream mass media, including television programmes, films, and music (Barker, Bowes-Catton, Iantaffi, Cassidy, & Brewer, 2008; Johnson, 2016). The invisibility and misrepresentation of bisexual and pansexual (and asexual and plurisexual) people in mainstream mass media matter (Corey, 2017; Gamson, 1998; Johnson, 2016). Media portrayals have the potential to shape our understandings of particular groups of people and can sometimes be the only representations that heterosexual people see of diverse sexualities, because they are often invisible within the wider culture (Gamson, 1998; Johnson, 2016).

The US-based organisation GLAAD (formally the Gay and Lesbian Alliance Against Defamation; now branded simply as GLAAD) monitors the media with the aim of working towards LGBTQ acceptance and inclusion. It has recently made explicit its inclusion of trans and asexual people, and has extended bisexuality to bisexual+ people (defined as those attracted to more than one gender, including bisexual, pansexual, fluid, queer, and more). Its most recent analysis indicates minimal or limited representations of diverse sexualities on television (Box 5.3).

BOX 5.3 THE (LACK OF) INCLUSION OF BISEXUAL, PAN-SEXUAL, AND ASEXUAL CHARACTERS ON TELEVISION

GLAAD's 2018 US-based analysis of sexuality on broadcast, cable, and streamed television reported that bisexual+ characters made up 27% of recurring LGBTQ characters – a 1% decrease on the previous year's report. Hence, bisexuality+ continued to be under-represented as an overall percentage of the LGBTQ population. Of these characters, 75 were women, 18 were men (hence bisexual+ women continued to be somewhat more represented than men), and two were trans. While there had been an overall increase in trans characters they only constituted 6% of the 433 recurring LGBTQ characters, and therefore trans people remained under-represented. Further, trans people's sexuality was often omitted, perhaps reflecting a conflation of gender and sexuality. GLAAD noted that (what was at the time a forthcoming series) *Chilling Adventures of Sabrina* would include a pansexual character (which it now does). For the second year in a row, they also identified only two asexual characters – one in *Shadowhunters*, and another in *BoJack Horseman*. Bisexual+ characters were mainly on cable channels, and harmful tropes continued to dominate. Bisexual+ characters were often depicted as untrustworthy, obsessive, lacking morals, and sexually manipulative. GLAAD campaigns for representations which avoid relying on stereotypes and instead capture the nuance and depth of bisexual+ identities (GLAAD, 2018).

More recently, diverse sexualities may be becoming somewhat more represented within some forms of mainstream mass media than they were in the past. Lists of fictional characters who are interpreted (or occasionally named) as pansexual or asexual can be found on the Internet. Lists of asexual characters mention Sheldon Cooper from the television sitcom *The Big Bang Theory*, Raphael Santiago in the television drama *Shadowhunters: The Mortal Instruments*, and Brad from the comedy series *Faking it* (Casano, 2018). Pansexual characters have more recently also been included in films, for example, Lando Calrissian in the 2018 film *Solo: A Star Wars Story*, Oberyn Martell and Yara Greyjoy in the fantasy series *Game of Thrones*, and the Marvel comic character Deadpool (Roget, 2018).

The representation of bisexual, pansexual, asexual, and plurisexual television characters and celebrities

Bisexual (and pansexual, asexual, and plurisexual) characters have often been absent from television. When they are included, their identities often remain unnamed, and/or they may be represented in a number of problematic ways (for examples, see Boxes 5.4 and 5.5, below). Scholars have highlighted how binary understandings of sexuality dominate. These perpetuate the erasure and invisibility of bisexuality, and of other identities involving attraction to more than one sex/gender:

> Fictional characters tend to be presented as straight if in a relationship with someone of the "opposite sex," and gay if in a relationship with someone of the "same sex." If someone becomes attracted to a person of a different gender to the one he or she was before, that someone is portrayed as changing from straight to gay (or vice versa).
>
> *(Barker et al., 2008, p. 145)*

Even if a character might be read as bisexual (or pansexual, asexual, or plurisexual), their sexuality is rarely overtly named as such. Characters' sexualities are often interpreted on the basis of their relationship behaviours (Barker et al., 2008; Wilde, 2015). Many portrayals of sexualities outside the heterosexual/homosexual binary therefore rely on non-monogamy, threesomes, love triangles, or short-lived casual relationships with people of different genders. These depictions risk shoring up stereotypes of bisexual (and pansexual and plurisexual) people, rather than capturing the diversity of those who identify with these sexualities (Amy-Chinn, 2012; Wilde, 2015; see also Box 5.4). Characters may be portrayed as promiscuous, hedonistic, unstable, abnormal, mentally ill, immoral, or even as murderers. Overall, representations of attraction to more than one gender are often largely negative. These characteristics are often specifically associated with the character's sexuality, and the take-home message is that bisexual (or pansexual or plurisexual) people – whether their sexuality is explicitly named or not – are destructive and a threat (Alexander, 2007; Johnson, 2016). While self-identifying asexual characters remain minimally represented on television, recent portrayals of asexuality may be less reliant on misconceptions and more validating of asexuality than those in the early 2000s (Tokheim, 2018; also see discussion below on asexual people's perceptions of representations in the media).

Media representations of bisexual characters vary according to gender. Bisexual women are more visible than bisexual men, but representations are often highly sexualised, and far from realistic (Johnson, 2016). If bisexual men are depicted at all, their sexuality is often effectively erased. They may be shown questioning whether they might be bisexual, only to later decide they are gay. Alternatively, they may be represented as engaging in unsafe sexual activities with multiple partners, and as having sexually transmitted infections, including

HIV. These characters therefore fit with notions of bisexual people as promiscuous and the vectors of disease (Alexander, 2007; Callis, 2013; Johnson, 2016). The overall lack of bisexual (and pansexual, asexual, and plurisexual) representations, and the oversexualised portrayals of women, may be partly attributable to the dominance of heterosexual men in influential roles (e.g., as writers, producers, and directors) (Johnson, 2016). Similar representations may feature in advertisements in mainstream media. In one analysis, bisexual characters made up only 2% of the 350 LGBT characters in advertisements (Nölke, 2018). These White middle-class men were shown as flirtatious, promiscuous, cheats, or daredevils. However, more recent adverts may be more positive and relate to a narrative of "love is love" regardless of the gender of the person one is attracted to (Nölke, 2018, p. 240).

BOX 5.4 FEMALE SEXUALITY IN *ORANGE IS THE NEW BLACK*

In 2017, US scholar Sarah Corey analysed representations of female bisexuality on television, including in the popular Netflix programme *Orange is the New Black*. It tells the story of Piper, who is established early in the show as having had relationships with men and women. The viewer's attention is drawn to Piper's attraction to, and behaviours with, more than one gender. However, she repeatedly avoids self-identification. Piper refers to the Kinsey scale and sexuality on a spectrum, but her identity is not explicitly named. Corey highlights that to name identities gives them credibility, whereas not doing so shores up notions that identity is binary, which perpetuates bisexual (and pansexual and plurisexual) invisibility. Piper's resistance to naming her own sexuality could be interpreted as due to her being confused or unable to make up her mind about her identity. The character arguably risks perpetuating these, and other stereotypical, beliefs about those who are attracted to more than one gender. When she rekindles her sexual relationship with ex-girlfriend Alex, she hides this from her husband Larry, to whom she is still married. This feeds into notions that those who are attracted to multiple genders are unable to be satisfied with one partner, cannot be monogamous, and will inevitably cheat. Piper is also selfish and lacks many redeeming qualities. Hence this portrayal of a character who has attractions to, and behaviours with, more than one gender is mainly negative (Corey, 2017).

BOX 5.5 MALE SEXUALITY IN *TORCHWOOD*

A rare example of a man being portrayed as an out and open bisexual person is the character of Captain Jack Harkness, in the BBC programme *Doctor Who* and the spin-off series *Torchwood* (Johnson, 2016). Jack has often been reported to be bisexual, including by lead writer and executive producer Russell

T. Davies, and by John Barrowman, the actor who plays him (see Barker et al., 2008; Knight, 2010). He has also been interpreted as pansexual or omnisexual, based on his attraction, love, and desire for anyone, including other species (Wilde, 2015). There have been positive reactions to the inclusion of a bisexual, pansexual, or omnisexual character, and this is particularly valued given the programme's high viewing figures (Amy-Chinn, 2012; Johnson, 2016; Wilde, 2015). However, it has been noted that the rarity of such characters makes the portrayal all the more critical, and the character is not entirely unproblematic (Johnson, 2016). While Jack is a "good guy", he is also a con man, and his sexuality is intertwined with notions of promiscuity (Barker et al., 2008; Johnson, 2016). Some have suggested that Jack's desires and reminiscences about his past mainly relate to male partners, so viewers might easily draw on conventional binary understandings of sexuality and read him as a gay man. However, others have highlighted the ongoing indications of Jack's attraction to same-sex/gender and different-sex/gender humans and aliens (Knight, 2010; Wilde, 2015).

Bisexual (and pansexual, asexual, and plurisexual) celebrities are also somewhat invisible or invalidated. Celebrities who now have same-sex/gender relationships but have a previous history of mainly different-sex/gender relationships are often assumed to now be gay. The possibility of bisexuality (or pansexuality or plurisexualities) is rarely considered or taken seriously (McLean, 2008; see also Box 5.6). Some celebrities have explicitly self-identified as bisexual. Those who gain media attention as a result of their public declarations tend to be women – for example, US pop singer Lady Gaga, and US actor Angelina Jolie. There is potential for increased bisexual visibility through their celebrity status, but this has remained unfulfilled, partly because stereotypes of bisexuality (e.g., as attention-seeking) are exacerbated in media interpretations (Capulet, 2010).

BOX 5.6 TOM DALEY AND THE ERASURE OF THE POSSIBILITY OF BISEXUALITY

While there have been some openly gay and lesbian athletes, there remain few high-profile elite sportspeople who are out as bisexual, pansexual, asexual, or plurisexual. In 2013, British Olympic diver Tom Daley (who has celebrity status in the UK) announced on social media that he was dating a man. He also mentioned that he had previously dated women and "still fancied girls". According to an analysis of 43 print media articles and editorials published in British newspapers following Daley's announcement (Magrath et al., 2017), the majority stated that he was a gay athlete, a gay man, or in a gay relationship. Despite his declaration that he was still attracted to women, only four articles explicitly mentioned that he might be bisexual. Hence, the possibility of bisexuality, pansexuality, or other plurisexualities was largely overlooked. There may be various reasons why Daley chose not to name his identity. He may not have felt that labels were important to him, which would reflect a wider cultural turn away from embracing labelling. He may have felt that his statement about being attracted to women made his bisexuality (or pansexuality or plurisexuality) apparent. Alternatively, he may have stated that he was still interested in women to maintain his fan base – which likely includes women who are attracted to men. Since then, he has self-identified as gay in one of his YouTube videos. However, he has also stated in an interview that he does not label himself but still has sexual feelings towards women.

Celebrity status remains one potential strategy for overcoming the erasure and invisibility of bisexual, pansexual, asexual, and plurisexual people. Most recently, some celebrities have declared their pansexuality, to generally positive responses. These have included US singers Miley Cyrus and Brendon Urie, who have discussed their pansexuality, and British comedian Joe Lycett, who has spoken publicly of his sexuality (initially as bisexual, and more recently as pansexual) (Montgomery, 2019).

Bisexual, pansexual, asexual, and plurisexual people's perceptions of media representations

Minimal research has asked bisexual, asexual, pansexual, or plurisexual people about their perceptions of sexuality in the media. However, in the US, over 600 bisexual participants (mainly White cisgender women between 18 and 34 years old) responded to a survey of how bisexuality was represented in the media. Most reported that media portrayals were negative (46.5%) or somewhat negative (35.7%), and those who had been diagnosed with a mental disorder were significantly more likely to select these options. The author argues that media representation may have a part to play in perpetuating biphobia within the wider culture, which in turn might contribute to poor mental health among bisexual (and perhaps pansexual, asexual, and plurisexual) people (Johnson, 2016).

In a US study (Rothblum et al., 2019), asexual participants noted that there were few asexual characters in the media. One participant highlighted that a character in the medical drama *Grey's Anatomy* had declared that they had no sex drive, only for this to be dismissed as impossible by a health professional. The character was later diagnosed with a brain tumour, which was used to explain away their asexuality. The participant reported that, although the word asexual was not used, this portrayal was nonetheless unhelpful. Another participant highlighted that positive representations of asexuality would not only be welcome, but could potentially reduce some asexual people's sense of isolation. Other representations of asexuality were discussed more positively, including the likeable character of Todd in the comedy-drama *BoJack Horseman* (Rothblum et al., 2019; see also Tokheim, 2018). To date, most seemingly asexual characters have been men, who are often shown as geeky/nerdy, such as Sheldon Cooper in *The Big Bang Theory* (Gupta, 2019; Tokheim, 2018). The recent development of the geek/nerd as holding some cultural capital may mean that such portrayals enable some acceptance of asexuality (see Gupta, 2019), albeit only a particular version of asexual people. One participant discussed how meaningful it was for them to see an asexual character who was in a romantic relationship and who defied stereotypes of asexual people as "unfeeling robots who are also nerds or something" (Rothblum et al., 2019, p. 91). It remains critical that writers, directors, and producers ensure that representations of asexual characters include women and do not become limited to certain tropes.

It can be empowering to see our own identities affirmatively represented, and positive portrayals of bisexual (and pansexual, asexual, and plurisexual) characters and celebrities in the media hold the potential to help reduce misunderstandings and phobias (Gamson, 1998). For bisexual, pansexual, asexual, and plurisexual people, positive representations may also make them feel that their identity is acceptable and valid (e.g., Johnson, 2016; Tokheim, 2018). However, there is a risk that when diverse sexualities become more visible within the media, some portrayals make bisexuality, pansexuality, and plurisexual identities seem even less valid or viable than when they were overlooked (Callis, 2013; Capulet, 2010). In turn, poor media representations may also impact negatively on bisexual, pansexual, asexual, and plurisexual people's well-being (Johnson, 2016; Rothblum et al., 2019).

In this chapter, some key themes were identified. In schools, workplaces, and mainstream mass media, bisexual, pansexual, asexual, and plurisexual people are often invisible. This invisibility arises from binary understandings of sexuality and the overlooking or lack of meaningful inclusion of diverse sexualities. If bisexual, pansexual, asexual, and plurisexual identities become visible, they are often understood or represented in limited, often stereotypical ways. Misunderstandings and dismissals of bisexuality, pansexuality, asexuality, and plurisexualities not only make it particularly challenging for people with diverse sexualities to be out and open but also significantly impact on their experiences of school, work, and their wider lives.

References

Alexander, J. (2007). Bisexuality in the media: A digital roundtable. *Journal of Bisexuality*, 7(1–2), 113–124. doi:10.1300/J159v07n01_07

Amy-Chinn, D. (2012). GLAAD to be Torchwood? Bisexuality and the BBC. *Journal of Bisexuality*, 12(1), 63–79. doi:10.1080/15299716.2012.645719

Barker, M. (2007). Heteronormativity and the exclusion of bisexuality in psychology. In V. Clarke, & E. Peel (Eds.), *Out in psychology: Lesbian, gay, bisexual, trans, and queer perspectives* (pp. 86–118). Chichester: John Wiley & Sons.

Barker, M., Bowes-Catton, H., Iantaffi, A., Cassidy, A., & Brewer, L. (2008). British bisexuality: A snapshot of bisexual representations and identities in the United Kingdom. *Journal of Bisexuality, 8*(1–2), 141–162. doi:10.1080/15299710802143026

Bisexual Issues Committee. (2018, September 27). *Being bi in psychology: The importance of visibility and validation.* Washington, DC: Bisexual Issues Committee of Division 44: Society for the Psychology of Sexual Orientation and Gender Diversity.

Bowen, F., & Blackmon, K. (2003). Spirals of silence: The dynamic effects of diversity on organizational voice. *Journal of Management Studies, 40*(6), 1393–1417. doi:10.1111/1467-6486.00385

Buchanan, N. T., & Settles, I. H. (2019). Managing (in)visibility and hypervisibility in the workplace. *Journal of Vocational Behaviour, 113*, 1–5. doi:10.1016/j.jvb.2018.11.001

Callis, A. S. (2013). The black sheep of the pink flock: Labels, stigma, and bisexual identity. *Journal of Bisexuality, 13*(1), 82–105. doi:10.1080/15299716.2013.755730

Capulet, I. (2010). With reps like these: Bisexuality and celebrity status. *Journal of Bisexuality, 10*(3), 294–308. doi:10.1080/15299716.2010.500962

Carpenter, C. (2008). Sexual orientation, income, and non-pecuniary economic outcomes: New evidence from young lesbians in Australia. *Review of Economics of the Household, 6*(4), 391–408. doi:10.1007/s11150-008-9034-5

Casano, A. (2018). Fictional characters who are asexual. Retrieved from www.ranker.com/list/fictional-characters-who-are-asexual/anncasano

Chamberlain, B. (2009/2012). *Bisexual people in the workplace: Practical advice for employers.* London: Stonewall.

Clair, J. A., Beatty, J. E., & MacLean, T. L. (2005). Out of sight but not out of mind: Managing invisible social identities in the workplace. *Academy of Management Review, 30*(1), 78–95. doi:10.5465/amr.2005.15281431

Compton, C. A., & Dougherty, D. S. (2017). Organizing sexuality: Silencing and the push-pull process of co-sexuality in the workplace. *Journal of Communication, 67*(6), 874–896. doi:10.1111/jcom.12336

Connell, C. (2012). Dangerous disclosures. *Sexuality Research and Social Policy, 9*(2), 168–177. doi:10.1007/s13178-011-0076-8

Corey, S. (2017). All bi myself: Analyzing television's presentation of female bisexuality. *Journal of Bisexuality, 17*(2), 190–205. doi:10.1080/15299716.2017.1305940

D'Allaird, C. J. (2016). *Who feels included at work? Intersectionality and perceptions of diversity and inclusion in the workplace* (Unpublished master's dissertation). State University of New York, Albany.

Dixon, J., & Dougherty, D. S. (2014). A language convergence/meaning divergence analysis exploring how LGBTQ and single employees manage traditional family expectations in the workplace. *Journal of Applied Communication Research, 42*(1), 1–19. doi:10.1080/00909882.2013.847275

Elia, J. P. (2010). Bisexuality and school culture: School as a prime site for bi-intervention. *Journal of Bisexuality, 10*(4), 452–471. doi:10.1080/15299716.2010.521060

Epstein, D. (2000). Sexualities and education: Catch 28. *Sexualities, 3*(4), 387–394. doi:10.1177/136346000003004001

Formby, E. (2017). How should we "care" for LGBT+ students within higher education? *Pastoral Care in Education, 35*(3), 203–220. doi:10.1080/02643944.2017.1363811

Francis, D. A. (2017). "I think we had one or two of those, but they weren't really": Teacher and learner talk on bisexuality in South African schools. *Journal of Bisexuality, 17*(2), 206–224. doi:10.1080/15299716.2017.1326998

Gamson, J. (1998). Publicity traps: Television talk shows and lesbian, gay, bisexual, and transgender visibility. *Sexualities*, *1*(1), 11–41. doi:10.1177/136346098001001002

Gegenfurtner, A., & Gebhardt, M. (2017). Sexuality education including lesbian, gay, bisexual, and transgender (LGBT) issues in schools. *Educational Research Review*, *22*, 215–222. doi:10.1016/j.edurev.2017.10.002

GLAAD. (2018). 2018–2019: Where we are on TV. Retrieved from http://glaad.org/files/WWAT/WWAT_GLAAD_2018-2019.pdf

Green, H. B., Payne, N. R., & Green, J. (2011). Working bi: Preliminary findings from a survey on workplace experiences of bisexual people. *Journal of Bisexuality*, *11*(2–3), 300–316. doi:10.1080/15299716.2011.572007

Greenland, K., & Nunney, R. (2008). The repeal of Section 28: It ain't over 'til it's over. *Pastoral Care in Education*, *26*(4), 243–251. doi:10.1080/02643940802472171

Gupta, K. (2019). Gendering asexuality and asexualizing gender: A qualitative study exploring the intersections between gender and asexuality. *Sexualities*, *22*(7–8), 1197–1216. doi:10.1177/1363460718790890

Harding, R., & Peel, E. (2007). Heterosexism at work: Diversity training, discrimination law and the limits of liberal individualism. In V. Clarke, & E. Peel (Eds.), *Out in psychology: Lesbian, gay, bisexual, trans, and queer perspectives* (pp. 247–271). Chichester: John Wiley & Sons.

Hillier, L., & Mitchell, A. (2008). "It was as useful as a chocolate kettle": Sex education in the lives of same-sex-attracted young people in Australia. *Sex Education*, *8*(2), 211–224. doi:10.1080/14681810801981258

Johnson, H. J. (2016). Bisexuality, mental health, and media representation. *Journal of Bisexuality*, *16*(3), 378–396. doi:10.1080/15299716.2016.1168335

Jones, T., & Hillier, L. (2014). The erasure of bisexual students in Australian education policy and practice. *Journal of Bisexuality*, *14*(1), 53–74. doi:10.1080/15299716.2014.872465

Kehoe, K. P. (2018). *Entitled snowflakes with student loans and side hustles: Media governmentality and the paradoxical construction of the millennial generation* (Unpublished doctoral thesis). California State University, Long Beach.

Kennedy, K. G., & Fisher, E. S. (2010). Bisexual students in secondary schools: Understanding unique experiences and developing responsive practices. *Journal of Bisexuality*, *10*(4), 472–485. doi:10.1080/15299716.2010.521061

Knight, D. (2010, August 8). More Torchwood details revealed. Retrieved from web.archive.org/web/20110414165618/www.atvnewsnetwork.co.uk/today/index.php/atv-today/3540-more-torchwood-details-revealed

Köllen, T. (2013). Bisexuality and diversity management: Addressing the B in LGBT as a relevant "sexual orientation" in the workplace. *Journal of Bisexuality*, *13*(1), 122–137. doi:10.1080/15299716.2013.755728

Kosciw, J. G., Greytak, E. A., Giga, N. M., Villenas, C., & Danischewski, D. J. (2016). *The 2015 national school climate survey: The experiences of lesbian, gay, bisexual, transgender, and queer youth in our nation's schools*. New York: GLSEN.

Kuyper, L. (2015). Differences in workplace experiences between lesbian, gay, bisexual, and heterosexual employees in a representative population study. *Psychology of Sexual Orientation and Gender Diversity*, *2*(1), 1–11. doi:10.1037/sgd0000083

Lapointe, A. A. (2017). "It's not pans, it's people": Student and teacher perspectives on bisexuality and pansexuality. *Journal of Bisexuality*, *17*(1), 88–107. doi:10.1080/15299716.2016.1196157

Leppel, K. (2014). Does job satisfaction vary with sexual orientation? *Industrial Relations: A Journal of Economy and Society*, *53*(2), 169–198. doi:10.1111/irel.12053

Levitt, H. M., & Ippolito, M. R. (2014). Being transgender: Navigating minority stressors and developing authentic self-presentation. *Psychology of Women Quarterly, 38*(1), 46–64. doi:10.1177/0361684313501644

Lloren, A., & Parini, L. (2017). How LGBT-supportive workplace policies shape the experience of lesbian, gay men, and bisexual employees. *Sexuality Research and Social Policy, 14*(3), 289–299. doi:10.1007/s13178-016-0253-x

Magrath, R., Cleland, J., & Anderson, E. (2017). Bisexual erasure in the British print media: Representation of Tom Daley's coming out. *Journal of Bisexuality, 17*(3), 300–317. doi:10.1080/15299716.2017.1359130

McAllum, M. A. (2014). "Bisexuality is just semantics … ": Young bisexual women's experiences in New Zealand secondary schools. *Journal of Bisexuality, 14*(1), 75–93. doi:10.1080/15299716.2014.872467

McAllum, M. A. (2018). Young bisexual women's experiences in secondary schools: "Not everyone's straight so why are they only teaching that?". *Sex Education, 18*(3), 253–267. doi:10.1080/14681811.2017.1369024

McLean, K. (2007). Hiding in the closet? Bisexuals, coming out and the disclosure imperative. *Journal of Sociology, 43*(2), 151–166. doi:10.1177/1440783307076893

McLean, K. (2008). Silences and stereotypes: The impact of (mis)constructions of bisexuality on Australian bisexual men and women. *Gay and Lesbian Issues and Psychology Review, 4*(3), 158–165.

Montgomery, H. (2019, June 19). How pop culture embraced sexuality "without labels". Retrieved from www.bbc.com/culture/story/20190618-how-pop-culture-embraced-sexuality-without-labels

Nölke, A. I. (2018). Making diversity conform? An intersectional, longitudinal analysis of LGBT-specific mainstream media advertisements. *Journal of Homosexuality, 65*(2), 224–255. doi:10.1080/00918369.2017.1314163

Pew Research Center. (2013). *A survey of LGBT Americans: Attitudes, experiences and values in changing times.* Washington, DC: Author. Retrieved from www.pewsocialtrends.org/files/2013/06/SDT_LGBT-Americans_06-2013.pdf

Popova, M. (2018). Inactionable/unspeakable: Bisexuality in the workplace. *Journal of Bisexuality, 18*(1), 54–66. doi:10.1080/15299716.2017.1383334

Rasmussen, M. L. (2004). The problem of coming out. *Theory into Practice, 43*(2), 144–150. doi:10.1207/s15430421tip4302_8

Rivers, I. (2004). Recollections of bullying at school and their long-term implications for lesbians, gay men, and bisexuals. *Crisis, 25*(4), 169–175. doi:10.1027/0227-5910.25.4.169

Rivers, I. (2011). Narratives of marginalisation: The legacy of homophobia at school. *International Journal of Adolescence and Youth, 16*(2), 157–177. doi:10.1080/02673843.2011.9748053

Rivers, I. (2018). Homophobic, biphobic, and transphobic bullying in schools. In H. Cowie, & C. Myers (Eds.), *School bullying and mental health: Risks, intervention and prevention* (pp. 35–45). New York: Routledge.

Rivers, I., Gonzalez, C., Nodin, N., Peel, E., & Tyler, A. (2018). LGBT people and suicidality in youth: A qualitative study of perceptions of risk and protective circumstances. *Social Science & Medicine, 212*, 1–8. doi:10.1016/j.socscimed.2018.06.040

Roget, S. (2018). Pansexual characters in fiction. Retrieved from www.ranker.com/list/pansexual-characters-fiction/stephanroget

Rothblum, E. D., Heimann, K., & Carpenter, K. (2019). The lives of asexual individuals outside of sexual and romantic relationships: Education, occupation, religion and community. *Psychology & Sexuality, 10*(1), 83–93. doi:10.1080/19419899.2018.1552186

Ruggs, E. N., Martinez, L. R., Hebl, M. R., & Law, C. L. (2015). Workplace "trans"-actions: How organizations, coworkers, and individual openness influence perceived gender identity discrimination. *Psychology of Sexual Orientation and Gender Diversity, 2*(4), 404–412. doi:10.1037/sgd0000112

See, H., & Hunt, R. (2011). Bisexuality and identity: The double-edged sword: Stonewall research into bisexual experience. *Journal of Bisexuality, 11*(2–3), 290–299. doi:10.1080/15299716.2011.571995

Sterzing, P. R., Gartner, R. E., Goldbach, J. T., McGeough, B. L., Ratliff, G. A., & Johnson, K. C. (2019). Polyvictimization prevalence rates for sexual and gender minority adolescents: Breaking down the silos of victimization research. *Psychology of Violence, 9*(4), 419–430. doi:10.1037/vio0000123

Tokheim, D. J. (2018). *When the invisible become visible: How asexuality is represented in popular culture* (Unpublished master's dissertation). San Francisco State University, San Francisco.

TUC. (2019). *Sexual harassment of LGBT people in the workplace.* London: Author.

Tweedy, A. E. (2010). Polyamory as a sexual orientation. *University of Cincinnati Law Review, 79*(4), 1461–1515.

Walker, J., & Bates, J. (2016). Developments in LGBTQ provision in secondary school library services since the abolition of Section 28. *Journal of Librarianship and Information Science, 48*(3), 269–283. doi:10.1177/0961000614566340

Wilde, J. (2015). Gay, queer, or dimensional? Modes of reading bisexuality on Torchwood. *Journal of Bisexuality, 15*(3), 414–434. doi:10.1080/15299716.2014.1000473

Williams, C., & Giuffre, P. (2011). From organizational sexuality to queer organizations: Research on homosexuality and the workplace. *Sociology Compass, 5*(7), 551–563. doi:10.1111/j.1751-9020.2011.00392.x

6

BECOMING VISIBLE AND REFLECTING ON VISIBILITY

In this book the focus has been on the ways in which bisexual, pansexual, asexual, and plurisexual people tend to be largely invisible. If they do become visible, they are often marginalised, their identity invalidated, and their sexuality dismissed to the extent that it becomes invisible once more. This final chapter focuses on the ways in which bisexual, pansexual, asexual, and plurisexual people have become somewhat less invisible than they were in the past. What underpins some of this visibility is individuals sharing their sexuality with others in various ways. In doing so they personally become visible, which increases awareness of the existence of their identities among those to whom they have disclosed. Bisexual activists and allies have also been devoted to increasing the wider visibility of bisexuality and bisexual people, and this is also the case for asexuality and pansexuality to some extent. Where only particular identities are discussed in the source materials, I cite those mentioned in the texts. I also include in parentheses diverse sexualities to which the content might potentially extend, in order to both acknowledge them and note the lack of focus specifically on them. The chapter ends with some final reflections on visibility.

Making sexuality visible: Why might people not disclose to others?

Coming out has been recommended as a key strategy to increase the visibility of marginalised identities, and it has been suggested that those who are not "out" as bisexual perpetuate their own invisibility (e.g., See & Hunt, 2011). Indeed, much of the content of this chapter relates to various ways that individuals have personally become visible to others. However, the extent to which people feel able to disclose or be open about their sexualities varies. There are many reasons why lesbian and gay people might not want – or feel able – to be out and open about their sexuality (see Rasmussen, 2004). The same can also be said for bisexual (and pansexual, asexual, and plurisexual) people (McLean, 2007). Indeed, surveys indicate that bisexual and pansexual people are less likely to be out than lesbian and gay people (Box 6.1). Few surveys include asexual or plurisexual identities.

BOX 6.1 HOW MANY PEOPLE ARE OUT AND OPEN ABOUT THEIR IDENTITIES?

A recent Stonewall/YouGov report found that less than half of LGBT people in the UK felt that they could be out about their identities to all members of their family. The report showed that 8% of lesbian and gay people, 14% of trans people, and 32% of bisexual people were not out to anyone in their family. Furthermore, 2% of gay men, 1% of lesbian women, 8% of bisexual women, and 30% of bisexual men felt unable to be open about their sexuality to any of their friends (Bachmann & Gooch, 2018). This is mirrored in the US, where young bisexual and pansexual people were less likely than lesbian women and gay men to be out to their family, their teachers, or their classmates (Andre et al., 2014). In Stonewall's 2011 research, fewer than half of bisexual people were out in British workplaces (See & Hunt, 2011; see also Chapter 5). In the US, seven out of ten bisexual people reported that "none" or "only a few" of the people they worked closely with knew that they were bisexual (Pew Research Center, 2013, p. 59). Despite perceptions of a climate of equality – particularly within the UK – it is evident that there are still some who feel unable to be out and open about their identities. Further, this climate may arguably be under threat within both the US (in relation to President Trump) and the UK (following Brexit) where LGBTQ+ and race-related hate crimes have increased in recent years (e.g., McCloskey, 2017; Townsend, 2016).

There is a coming-out or disclosure imperative within LGBTQ+ communities (although some have reported rejecting this imperative as an act of resistance; see Wandrey, Mosack, & Moore, 2015). This can mean that coming out is understood as compulsory (McLean, 2007; Rasmussen, 2004; see also Chapter 5). Coming out has been situated as a milestone in the identity development of those who identify as gay or lesbian. However, to position it as a milestone overlooks how coming out is an ongoing series of events, involving multiple disclosures. Further, few coming-out models include bisexuality (or pansexuality, asexuality, or plurisexualities) (Bartelt, Bowling, Dodge, & Bostwick, 2017; Cramer & Gilson, 1999; Maliepaard, 2018; Rivers & Gordon, 2010; Scherrer, Kazyak, & Schmitz, 2015). While coming out is an important part of becoming visible, it is crucial that the barriers to coming out are recognised. There are particular challenges and complexities to disclosing specific identities and combinations of multiple and intersecting identities (see Boxes 6.2 and 6.3). I discuss these before moving to the ways in which bisexual, pansexual, and asexual people have become somewhat more visible than in the past. It is imperative that coming out is not positioned as obligatory and that those who remain private about their sexuality are not condemned as dishonest or cowardly (Garvey et al., 2018; McLean, 2007; Rasmussen, 2004). Those who do feel able to be out can potentially contribute to increasing the visibility and validity of diverse sexualities. However, placing the emphasis on individuals to come out should not be the only strategy. Instead, the onus needs to also be on others to demonstrate their inclusivity and help create safe environments. In turn, this can not only increase visibility and support people in feeling validated, but also ensure that those who are bisexual, pansexual, asexual, and plurisexual feel more able to disclose their identities to others (see also Chapter 5).

BOX 6.2 THE CHALLENGES AND COMPLEXITIES OF BEING OUT AND OPEN AS BISEXUAL, PANSEXUAL, AND ASEXUAL

Those attracted to people of more than one gender may fear negative responses to coming out, due to awareness of other people's individual beliefs and broader cultural understandings of their sexualities. Therefore, they may be hesitant to come out, given the potential for, or previous experiences of, misunderstanding, disbelief, and/or dismissal (Bartelt et al., 2017; Brown & Lilton, 2019; McLean, 2007; Robbins, Low, & Query, 2016; Ross, Dobinson, & Eady, 2010; Scherrer et al., 2015; Wandrey et al., 2015). One impact of the dismissal of bisexuality is that those who are bisexual may not feel that they are entitled to come out as bisexual – or at least not until they have "proved" themselves by having had "sufficient" relationships with people of more than one gender (McLean, 2007; see also Chapter 1 on the rigid parameters others may apply to what constitutes a "real bisexual"). How others respond may be nuanced according to different identities. Pansexual people have reported how tiresome they find it to have to explain their sexuality, or respond to jokes about being attracted to saucepans (Lapointe, 2017). Asexual people have faced confusion, disbelief, unwelcome questions, and/or assumptions that they are in need of therapy (Robbins et al., 2016; Rothblum, Heimann, & Carpenter, 2019). Those who are biromantic, panromantic, or who identify with other asexual spectrum identities may face multiple forms of discrimination (e.g., reactions to their asexuality as well as encountering the responses that bisexual and pansexual people report more widely) (see Julia, 2016).

Those who use multiple identity terms may make particularly nuanced decisions. Some have reported that they choose the terms they use selectively, depending on how they anticipate others will respond. Some pansexual people may come out as bisexual because the latter may be better understood within some contexts, or by particular people (Lapointe, 2017).

Some bisexual people report that they have come out as gay or lesbian, because they think others will be better able to understand these identities than bisexuality (Scherrer et al., 2015; Wandrey et al., 2015). The relevance and value of coming out may also vary according to people's identities and their current relationship status, including the gender of a partner (e.g., Robbins et al., 2016; Scherrer et al., 2015; Wandrey et al., 2015). Further, the gender of a current partner will not necessarily reveal the identities of those who are bisexual and pansexual (and who identify with asexual spectrum identities), hence they may have to find more explicit ways to come out (Hayfield, Campbell, & Reed, 2018; See & Hunt, 2011). Finally, some may dislike labels, or not feel a need to tightly name and claim their identities, which in turn could impact on how out and open they are (Maliepaard, 2018; See & Hunt, 2011).

In sum, those who consider disclosing their identities navigate whether, how, how often, to whom, and to what extent to come out. Their decisions may be informed by how relevant they deem their sexuality to be, the situation they are in, and anticipation of others' responses (Knous, 2006; Maliepaard, 2018; McLean, 2007; Scherrer et al., 2015; Wandrey et al., 2015).

BOX 6.3 THE CHALLENGES AND COMPLEXITIES OF BEING OUT AND OPEN IN RELATION TO THE INTERSECTIONS OF MULTIPLE IDENTITIES

Those who occupy multiple marginalised identities may have particularly nuanced experiences of negotiating being out and open. Factors which intersect with sexuality, and which may make disclosure particularly complex, include gender, race, ethnicity, age, parenthood, physical and intellectual disabilities, social class, and faith.

In a study of LGBTQ+ people of Colour, participants reported that they feared particularly negative responses from family, including the risk of being threatened or disowned. Some who were queer and trans concealed both their sexuality and their trans identities from others (Ghabrial, 2017). However, it is important not to assume that families will necessarily be biphobic, homophobic, or transphobic. In a study of different age groups, bisexual men aged 18–23, including people of Colour, reported relatively positive responses and acceptance from others. In contrast, those in their 30s and 40s had experienced biphobic responses, or had not felt able to come out until late in their lives (McCormack, Anderson, & Adams, 2014).

In relation to parenthood, some bisexual parents were fearful that their children would face biphobia due to their bisexuality. This concern informed how and when they disclosed, including to their own children, and to their children's friends' parents (Bartelt et al., 2017). Bisexual parents have also reported not wanting to come out to their children because their perception was that it would mean talking about their sex lives with them (Maliepaard, 2018). Others saw their personal experience of bisexuality as advantageous for them as parents, precisely because they were willing to discuss gender and sexuality, and were accepting of difference and diversity. Some parents felt that coming out did not feel relevant to them personally, but that it was a responsibility in order to raise awareness of the existence of bisexuality and act as an advocate (Bartelt et al., 2017).

Those who are disabled may find that others assume that they do not experience sexual feelings, or see them as deviant should they be open about having sexual desires (Kattari, 2014; Whitney, 2006). Those with intellectual disabilities have reported feeling insecure, anxious, lacking in verbal skills, and fearful of rejection in response to their coming out (Dinwoodie, Greenhill, & Cookson, 2016; Stoffelen, Schaafsma, Kok, & Curfs, 2018). For some, there may also be parallels between coming out as disabled and coming out as a particular sexuality – in relation to identity development, activism, community, and in/visibility (see Cramer & Gilson, 1999; Davies, 2000; Kattari, 2014; Whitney, 2006). These and other factors may all intersect and play a part in experiences of disclosure (e.g., Bachmann & Gooch, 2018; Bartelt et al., 2017; Garvey et al., 2018; Grov, Bimbi, Nanin, & Parsons, 2006).

Making sexuality visible by disclosing to friends, family, and others in person

Research indicates that many bisexual people want to come out in order to be honest, feel authentic, find support and acceptance, and become more visible as bisexual (e.g., Knous, 2006; McLean, 2007; Ross, Siegel, Dobinson, Epstein, & Steele, 2012). Disclosing one's own bisexuality can be beneficial in increasing the visibility and validity of bisexuality, not least because contact with bisexual people is related to more positive views of bisexuality and bisexual people (see Feinstein, Dyar, Bhatia, Latack, & Davila, 2016; Lytle, Dyar, Levy, & London, 2017). This may also apply to improving the visibility and validity of pansexuality, asexuality, and plurisexualities. There are various ways in which those with diverse sexualities can indicate or directly disclose their sexuality to others. Some may test the waters (e.g., by dropping hints about same-sex/gender attraction), to gauge what the response might be were they to disclose, or in the hope that others might work it out for themselves (McLean, 2007). While the gender of a bisexual person's current partner may not reveal their sexuality, some bisexual and pansexual people make reference to the genders of both current and previous partners, or discuss their multiple partners (although sharing that they are consensually non-monogamous/polyamorous adds further complexities) (Davila, Jabbour, Dyar, & Feinstein, 2019; Hayfield et al., 2018; McLean, 2007). Others have come out in the course of casual conversation, or by correcting false assumptions about the gender of their date (Wandrey et al., 2015) (although some bisexual and pansexual people may feel it is not worth the effort to correct others' misassumptions about their sexuality; see Brown & Lilton, 2019; McLean, 2007). Asexual people have reported coming out so that others understand that they are not looking for a relationship (although some asexual people may want to be in relationships). Some have reported that people's responses legitimised their identities (Robbins et al., 2016). Others come out using a range of strategies to ensure that their diverse sexualities are recognised.

Making sexuality visible through Pride symbols

The image of the rainbow, particularly on flags, has been widely recognised as a symbol of lesbian and gay pride. The rainbow flag offers opportunities for affiliation, solidarity, community, and pride, and is also a way in which identities can be made visible. The Pride flag was first designed by Gilbert Baker in 1978 (Wolowic, Heston, Saewyc, Porta, & Eisenberg, 2017). Each horizontal stripe of colour has a meaning (red for life; orange for healing; yellow for the sun; green for nature; blue for art; indigo for harmony; violet for spirit) (Andrews, 2017). The rainbow flag has to some extent been understood to be shared by those who are bisexual and trans – and more recently by a broader range of diverse identities. In 2018, an additional chevron was added to the flag, which includes black and brown stripes to represent people of Colour, and pink, pale blue, and white stripes to represent trans identities (Hitti, 2018).

Somewhat less recognised are flags specific to bisexuality, pansexuality, asexuality, asexual spectrum identities, and other sexualities (Table 6.1). Some bisexual people felt disconnected from the rainbow flag and wanted a universal symbol for bisexuality. The bisexual flag was first developed in 1998 with the specific intent of increasing the visibility of bisexual people, by Michael Page (Baxter-Williams, 2015). In 2010, the pansexual flag was developed, initially anonymously, by Instagram user JustJasper (JustJasper, 2013; Ruocco, 2014). In the same year, the asexual flag came about, following a competition led by the Asexuality Visibility and Education Network (AVEN), where members of online asexual communities submitted their designs (Asexuality Archive, 2012). There is also an ever-increasing range of flags which aim to capture people's asexual spectrum identities (see *My Umbrella* on the e-resources tab of this book's Routledge webpage).

A vast range of flags are becoming increasingly visible at Pride events, on the Internet, and in the wider culture. These can increase visibility and validity in various ways, for example, when individuals display flags on their social media pages as a way to come out to others, or when worn or waved at Pride events. They can also be used by practitioners and other service providers, who have included flags in their pamphlets, or displayed them in workplaces, to demonstrate that they are inclusive of diverse sexualities (Foster & Scherrer, 2014; Robbins et al., 2016; Scherrer, 2017).

TABLE 6.1 Pride flags

Flag	Year created	Colours and their meaning
Bisexual	1998	Pink – same-sex/gender attraction
		Blue – different-sex/gender attraction
		Purple – attraction to those who are the same sex/gender or a different sex/gender from oneself (Baxter-Williams, 2015)
Pansexual	2010	Pink – attraction to women/females/femininity
		Blue – attraction to men/males/masculinity
		Yellow – attraction to no gender/trans/non-binary/genderqueer people (JustJasper, 2013; Ruocco, 2014)
Asexual	2010	Black – to represent asexuality
		Grey – to represent grey and demisexual identities
		White – to represent non-asexual (allosexual) partners and allies
		Purple – to represent community (Asexuality Archive, 2012)

Making sexuality visible on the clothed body

In Chapter 4 the focus was on how there are seemingly few ways in which bisexual (and pansexual, asexual, and plurisexual) people can convey or communicate their sexuality through how they dress and appear. However, one way to somewhat more explicitly make sexualities visible on the body is to wear T-shirts and badges which explicitly state or otherwise indicate the wearer's sexuality (Box 6.4). To date, little research has explored this area and the extant literature has rarely included bisexual, pansexual, asexual, and plurisexual identities (for exceptions see Davila et al., 2019, whose participants included pansexual and queer people, and Hartman, 2013 on bisexual displays). Scholars have reported that shared codes and symbols of identity were used during the early lesbian and gay rights movement to identify others, come together, build communities, and campaign for social and political recognition and rights (Penney, 2013). Since the decriminalisation of same-sex sexual acts, and within somewhat less disapproving and discriminatory climates, lesbian and gay people have drawn on more explicit symbols and declarations of sexuality (Penney, 2013). Pride T-shirts offer opportunities to express and communicate sexuality by labelling the body, making identities visible to others, functioning as a form of solidarity, and serving as an activist strategy for political advocacy (e.g., Clarke, 2016, 2019; Penney, 2013). *Wearing Gay History* is a digital project where thousands of examples of historical LGBT pride T-shirts can be viewed (see the e-resources tab of this book's Routledge webpage for the link).

BOX 6.4 BISEXUAL, PANSEXUAL, AND ASEXUAL T-SHIRTS, BADGES, AND JEWELLERY

T-shirts and badges somewhat uniquely offer a way in which people can explicitly make their sexualities visible. An Internet search for bisexual, pansexual, or asexual T-shirts reveals an array of slogans, some of which draw on the colours of Pride flags. Pansexuality slogans include: *proud to be pansexual*; *hearts not parts*; *love knows no gender*; *pansexual pirate: likes all kinds of booty*; and *more pan than Peter and twice as magical.* Asexuality T-shirts are also available, including *asexual and proud*; *yes I'm asexual, no I'm not waiting to meet the right person*; *ace from space*; and *I'd rather eat cake.* Following online discussions of the lack of public visibility of asexuality, members of the asexual community initiated the wearing of a black ring on the right middle finger. This has become an established symbol of asexuality, which can allow asexual people "in the know" to potentially identify each other (Chasin, 2013; Nerin, 2015).

Bisexual slogans sometimes make direct statements about bisexual invisibility, such as *visiBIlity matters* and *total bi visibility.* Others (sometimes provocatively) explicitly challenge the denigration and dismissal of bisexuality (see Chapter 3). These include: *we are real*; *bisexuals exist*; *ain't no lie baby, bi bi bi!*; *bisexuals are not confused*; *bisexuals are confused (by your prejudice)*; *not confused, not greedy, bisexual*; *yes I'm still bisexual*; and *who I am is not determined by who I'm with.* Badges and buttons are also available, such as *your fence is sitting on me* and *no, I'm bisexual, you're confused* (see Jennifer Moore's Uncharted Worlds website). What many items have in common are proud declarations and statements which sometimes (often humorously) challenge misconceptions of sexualities. You can see links to the Internet sites where these slogans can be found on the e-resources tab of this book's Routledge webpage.

However, not everyone wants to wear clothes or badges to make explicit statements about sexuality. This partly links to how visibility can become vulnerability (e.g., they may not feel comfortable or safe enough to declare their sexuality so publicly). Further, wearing slogans cannot easily capture the fluidity of sexuality (Clarke, 2019). Further, as young people increasingly identify with multiple and increasingly diverse identities, T-shirts may not be tailored to everyone's specific identifications. Finally, declarations of sexuality via slogans may not be well received, particularly when they are understood as "too much" or "in your face" (Clarke, 2016, p. 6, Clarke, 2019). This may inform why so many statements are humorous – because playfulness and humour can serve to make the wearer seem more human, which in turn may make the message more readily acceptable (Penney, 2013). On the other hand, despite explicit statements of sexuality, others may not take the message at face value or may miss, or resist, the idea that the wearer is announcing their own sexuality (Hartman, 2013; Khayatt, 1997).

Making sexuality visible within the home

Another way in which people's identities may become visible is within their homes. Social and cultural geographer Andrew Gorman-Murray's research has focused extensively on how people's homes are personal and social as well as physical spaces. Therefore, our homes can come to represent our selves and our identities (e.g., Gorman-Murray, 2006, 2007, 2008, 2012, 2015). The homes which LGBTQ+ people grew up in are most likely to have been heterosexual spaces (although this is not always the case, and numbers of LBGTQ+ parents are ever increasing [Barefoot, Smalley, & Warren, 2017; Bartelt et al., 2017; Goldberg, 2010], with bisexual people more likely to be parents than gay or lesbian people [Goldberg, Gartrell, Nanette, & Gates, 2014]). Gorman-Murray analysed autobiographical narratives written by six lesbian women, six gay men, and one bisexual woman about their positive experiences of coming out to heterosexual parents while living at home. He identified the potential for the family home to become a space where heteronormativity could be subverted and LGB identities could become visible. This included through photographs of LGB people and their partners being displayed in the house and in what was watched on television. In these and other ways, our family homes, and our own living spaces, can be marked with our sexualities (Gorman-Murray, 2008). We might think of our homes as private, and allowing people into our space is contingent on various aspects; for example, some may feel fearful of others' surveillance. Nonetheless, there are possibilities for our personal space to become a public space. Neighbours might see our homes from outside, and we do tend to invite at least some other people to enter, many of whom may identify their sexuality in different ways from us (Gorman-Murray, 2012). In this sense, our living space may be one way in which our sexuality can become visible.

Homes and care homes may also be spaces which potentially offer opportunities for visibility and validation. As lesbian, gay, and bisexual (and pansexual, asexual, and plurisexual) people age, many will need others to care for them in their own homes, or will move into retirement or nursing homes. This is particularly relevant for older generations of LGBTQ+ people, who may be at higher risk of psychological and physical health disparities, due to factors associated with their gender and sexuality (Grigorovich, 2015). Care is often perceived by lesbians, gay men, and bisexual people to be predominantly heterosexual and heterosexist. This potentially perpetuates the invisibility of LGBTQ+ identities in people's own homes and within home care settings. Indeed, some LGBTQ+ older people have reported their fears about isolation due to lack of visibility and discussed the risks involved in becoming visible (Westwood, 2016; Willis, Maegusuku-Hewett, Raithby, & Miles, 2016). Older lesbian and bisexual women have spoken of carefully gauging the potential reactions of care workers, before gradually coming out to them. Some experience negative reactions, prejudice, and discrimination when they disclose, but others report positive responses (Grigorovich, 2015). While some researchers have included bisexual participants, there is a paucity of knowledge around the specificities of visibility and well-being in the context of caring for older bisexual people and this will also become relevant for pansexual, asexual, and plurisexual people as they get older.

Making sexuality visible on the web

The Internet is one place where sexualities and shared communities have become most visible and where there are key opportunities for validation – albeit amid a mass of information which may not be affirmative of these identities.

Blogs, videos, vlogs, and social media accounts

Some bisexual, pansexual, asexual, and plurisexual people use the Internet to find others like them and to come out within virtual spaces, some of which may be perceived as safe and supportive. To do so can increase their visibility and enable them to test how others might respond to them coming out in person (e.g., Lovelock, 2019). Blogs may be one way in which bisexual people can – potentially anonymously – explore their own identity, come out to others, share their experiences of being bisexual (and pansexual, asexual, and plurisexual), and seek support from those who comment. Others who read blogs could find them a useful resource when they themselves, or their friends and family, are coming out (George, 2011). Making their own YouTube videos or vlogs is another way in which bisexual (and pansexual, asexual, and plurisexual) people might come out (Lovelock, 2019). YouTube is one example of how consumers of visual culture have also become the producers of that culture (Schroer, 2014). Therefore, these videos allow people to make sense of and construct their own identities. They also offer opportunities for people to share their feelings and their experiences of their identities including of coming out to others in non-virtual spaces (Lovelock, 2019). YouTube videos also hold the potential for individuals to draw attention to themselves, which offers opportunities for greater social visibility (Schroer, 2014). Some bisexual video content indicates that those who created them may feel able to be more open in their videos than they are to people they know in person (Lovelock, 2019).

Another way in which people can come out, which may feel less risky than coming out face to face or via online video content, is through individual social media accounts. Bisexual, pansexual, asexual, and plurisexual people may utilise social media to come out directly (e.g., including their sexuality on their user profiles, announcing their identity in a post or status update, or via WhatsApp) or indirectly (e.g., by posting articles about their sexuality) (e.g., Davila et al., 2019; Maliepaard, 2018; Robbins et al., 2016). Other forms of online content which may raise the visibility and validity of diverse sexualities include comics, graphic novels, and zines (Box 6.5).

BOX 6.5 COMICS, GRAPHIC NOVELS, AND ZINES

One strategy used by activists, artists, and researchers to increase the visibility and validity of bisexual, pansexual, asexual, and plurisexual identities has been comics, graphic novels, and zines. For example, bisexual researcher Lisbeth Berbary and queer illustrator/artist Coco Guzman worked together to develop a comic called *We Exist: A Comic About Bisexuality*. Their aim was to help to combat bisexual erasure and challenge misconceptions about bisexuality. They conducted life story interviews with bisexual women in Canada to inform the content. Participants' stories included common experiences around navigating their identities, particularly within a social context where they encountered common cultural misunderstandings about bisexuality. The authors also focused on the intersections of identity in relation to race, religion, and other factors. The final version is designed to be printed as a comic zine and used as an educational resource for "peers, friends, family and colleagues" (Berbary & Guzman, 2018, p. 481).

Others have also utilised visual media and made their content publicly available on the Internet. In the UK, Meg-John Barker hosts *Rewriting the Rules*. This website consists of a range of materials, including free zines, which aim to provide accessible information on gender, sex, and relationship diversity through a distinctly intersectional lens. In the US, cartoonist Kori Michele Handwerker has written zines and comics around gender, sexuality, and identity – including bisexual and pansexual identities – in *Let's Talk About Bisexuality!*

Asexual community members Omnes et Nihil and Olivia M. have worked together to create a WordPress page dedicated to archiving ace zines. These zines focus on validating and supporting those who identify with asexual identities, and are educational for others. The list includes a huge range of intersectional topics, including race, religion, disability, and gender.

You can see links to the Internet sites relating to these projects on the e-resources tab of this book's Routledge webpage.

The existence of the Internet gives people various opportunities to express themselves, come out, seek support, and educate themselves. These self-produced formats increase the presence of bisexual, pansexual, asexual, and plurisexual content on the Internet, and hold the potential to contribute to increased visibility and validity of diverse sexualities.

Online communities, websites, networks, and campaigns

Online communities may play an important part in the lives of bisexual, pansexual, and asexual people and sometimes offer safe community spaces to be out and open about their sexualities. Websites, online networks, and campaigns established by activists and organisations also often aim to raise the visibility and validity of diverse sexualities (Davila et al., 2019). In one US study, some participants reported that they had been unaware of the existence of asexuality until they searched on the Internet. Online communities, AVEN in particular, were understood as particularly important for finding out about asexuality. Sometimes these were the only spaces in which asexual people felt able to come out, knowing that others would understand and were there to support and validate them. Some participants who had come out to friends and families had then directed them to online communities, so that they could learn more. Online communities therefore serve as a way to support asexual people and to direct others to spaces where they can become educated about asexuality (Robbins et al., 2016).

Indeed, there are many credible sources of education and advocacy available on the Internet. In the US, the Bisexual Resource Center is one of the longest-established organisations, founded by activists in the mid-1980s. Its aim is to support bi and bi+ people (defined as including pansexual, asexual, omnisexual, queer, fluid, and others), to build community, and to increase public awareness and visibility of bisexuality+. As the name suggests, its website contains many resources for bi+ people and their allies. The Bisexual Foundation/American Institute of Bisexuality has a website which aims to give a voice to bisexual people, raise the visibility of bisexuality, and promote understanding through education and awareness (see the e-resources tab of this book's Routledge webpage for links to these organisations). In recent years, there has been a turn towards the explicit inclusion of pansexuality and plurisexual identities on sites which were initially established in relation to bisexualities. This is important for working together to ensure that those with a wide range of diverse sexualities feel included, and that those with shared experiences are united rather than divided. For example, the *#StillBisexual* campaign was started in 2015 by bisexual activist Nicole Kristal (Compton, 2017; Gonzalez, Ramirez, & Galupo, 2017; see the e-resources tab of this book's Routledge webpage for a link). While the name only includes bisexuality, the site contains materials relating to pansexuality, asexualities, and fluid and queer identities. Alongside aiming to raise the visibility and validity of those who identify with bisexuality and plurisexual identities, the focus is on highlighting that these identities are ongoing for many people – whether they are single or in relationships (monogamous or consensually non-monogamous/polyamorous), and regardless of the gender(s) of their partner(s). Accordingly, the content of many of the confessional-style videos on the site is on challenging stereotypes and highlighting that sexuality can be enduring (Gonzalez et al., 2017). Bi Visibility Day has been celebrated on 23rd September every year since 1999, with the aim of increasing awareness of biphobia and the existence of bisexuality and bisexual communities (see the e-resources tab of this book's Routledge webpage for a link). More recently, Pansexual Visibility Day (May 24th) and Asexual Awareness Week (in late October) have also come into existence.

One final example is that of BiUK, created by Meg-John Barker and Christina Richards to "promote and support bisexuality research in the UK" and to develop links between academics and activists (see the e-resources tab of this book's Routledge webpage for a link). This endeavour led to the development of BiReCon and EuroBiReCon, both conferences at which academics, activists, and practitioners interested in bisexuality research can come together. These events create opportunities for working together and increasing the visibility of bisexuality, both in terms of their sheer existence, and in relation to the work that they do. In turn, the work of BiUK members led to the development of *The Bisexuality Report*, which has had a significant impact on the recognition of bisexuality, including within policy and practice (Barker, Richards, Jones, Bowes-Catton, & Plowman, 2012; Box 6.6).

BOX 6.6 THE BISEXUALITY REPORT (BARKER ET AL., 2012)

In 2012, UK academics and activists Meg-John Barker, Christina Richards, Helen Bowes-Catton, and Tracey Plowman wrote *The Bisexuality Report* with the aim of informing UK policy and practice. They highlighted the importance of specifically focusing on bisexuality, rather than amalgamating lesbian, gay, bisexual, and trans experiences. The report also drew attention to bisexual invisibility and exclusion within the media (see Chapter 5), lesbian and gay spaces (see Chapter 3), academia (see Chapter 1), and policy and legislation. The authors made a number of broad recommendations, placing the onus on those working with bisexual people to take action to ensure that bisexuality becomes more visible and validated. These recommendations included working with bisexual groups, organisations, and communities; ensuring that bisexual people and bisexuality were included at key events, within working groups, and in policies; and supporting research and other initiatives focused on bisexuality. They also made recommendations for specific sectors (e.g., education, the workplace, health settings, and so on). While the title was focused on bisexuality, their definition of what the term bisexual meant was broad (e.g., people who are attracted "to more than one gender", or who are attracted to others "regardless of gender", or whose identities are fluid; Barker et al., 2012, p. 3). Therefore, suggestions made in the report would extend to pansexual, asexual, and plurisexual identities. Since its official launch, *The Bisexuality Report* has been cited in academic work over 100 times, and has been recognised as a key resource for those working with bisexual people.

Making sexuality visible through offline communities

LGBTQ+ communities have been reported to be particularly important for people to find a safe space, come out, socialise, support each other, make friends, meet partners, and feel a sense of acceptance, belonging, and solidarity (e.g., Formby, 2012). Becoming visible was a key part of early lesbian and gay communities, movements, and activism (Box 6.7). It has been reported that some bisexual and pansexual people do not feel comfortable within wider LGBTQ+ communities (e.g., Formby, 2012; Hayfield, Clarke, & Halliwell, 2014). However, for others, being a part of LGBTQ+ communities and organisations, or participating in associated causes, is one way in which they might try to make their identity visible (Davila et al., 2019).

BOX 6.7 BECOMING VISIBLE AS A STRATEGY WITHIN LESBIAN AND GAY MOVEMENTS

In the 1950s and 1960s, the first social-political lesbian and gay organisations were founded (e.g., the Daughters of Bilitis, the Minorities Research Group, and the Mattachine Foundation/Society). These organisations met anonymously, and their names deliberately concealed the identities of their membership. Lesbians and gay men were stigmatised and faced a hostile climate, not least because same-sex acts were criminalised in many places. There was a risk of meetings being raided by police, of people losing their jobs or homes, or of them being attacked or imprisoned. Nonetheless, members were gradually encouraged to become visible to others in order to promote understanding and raise public awareness of lesbian and gay sexualities.

Initially, these organisations' strategies for the legitimisation and decriminalisation of homosexuality were mainly conservative and assimilationist (Bernstein, 2002; Meeker, 2001; Schultz, 2001). But by the mid-1960s and into the 1970s, lesbians and gay men (and bisexual people who were part of lesbian and gay movements) began to engage in more radical and liberatory politics. This was informed both by the sexual revolution of the 1960s, and by the strategies of other political movements (e.g., the civil rights and Black Power movements) (Bernstein, 2002; Meyer, 2006). The lesbian and gay rights movement began to engage in public protests (including at the Stonewall Inn in 1969), and generated publicity in its creation of a visible political movement. This visibility enabled gay men and lesbians to come out and unite in their demands for more radical changes in social and legal status (Meyer, 2006). Visibility has been an important strategy for LGBTQ+ people to create communities and champion equal rights.

Bisexual people began to mobilise and create specifically bisexual communities during the 1970s and 1980s, as discussed in Chapter 1. There are a number of bisexual communities in existence. In the UK, *Bi Community News* lists local groups and community events in its bimonthly printed magazine and on the Internet (see the e-resources tab of this book's Routledge webpage for a link). In 2019, the first bi Pride event was announced for those "who experience attraction beyond gender" (e.g., bi/bisexual/biromantic, pan/pansexual/panromantic, poly-sexual/polyromantic) to be visible and celebrate their identities at a dedicated event (see the e-resources tab of this book's Routledge webpage for a link). A range of local, national, and international bisexual community events also exist, such as BiFest. and the weekend-long BiCon (see the e-resources tab of this book's Routledge webpage for a link). First held in 1985, BiCon is an annual event which enables bisexual people (and their allies) to come out, connect with others, discuss their identities within a safe space, and be part of a community (Barker, Bowes-Catton, Iantaffi, Cassidy, & Brewer, 2008; Monro, 2015). Some have reported that attending BiCon was "life-changing" and "liberating" (Monro, 2015, pp. 36–37). However, LGBTQ+ and bisexual communities may not always feel accessible or inclusive to everyone (e.g., people of faith) and research partici-pants have reported incidents of ageism, disablism, and racism (Formby, 2012; Monro, 2015). The organisers of BiCon are keen to address these types of issues and are currently setting up working groups in relation to racism and access (Bi Community News, 2019). There are also bisexual groups such as Bi's (sic) of Colour, established in 2012, and organisations of people of faith and/or Colour which include bisexual people, such as Hidayah for LGBTQI+ Muslims and KeshetUK for Jewish LGBT people (see the e-resources tab of this book's Rou-tledge webpage for links to these organisations). These often aim to provide inclu-sive spaces, give people a voice, create communities, and work together for social change. These types of groups and events may play a significant part in providing a sense of community and creating opportunities to increase the visibility and val-idation of diverse sexualities through their existence and activities.

Some final reflections on in/visibility

This book has discussed the underpinnings of bisexual invisibility and offered a contemporary exploration of bisexual, pansexual, asexual, and plurisexual in/visibility within Western societies. It has documented the ways in which the work of first-wave and second-wave sexologists created the foundations of bisexual invisibility through binary and dichotomous models of sexuality. It has evidenced how bisexuality, pansexuality, asexuality, and plurisexualities have remained relatively overlooked within sexualities research (Chapters 1, 2, and 3). Bisexual, pansexual, asexual, and plurisexual people, and their identities, are often invisible to each other, and to those within the wider culture (Chapters 4 and 5). When bisexuality, and perhaps pansexuality, asexuality, and plurisexuali-ties, have become visible, they have often been denigrated or dismissed. This may reflect how when marginalised identities become visible, they are seen as a threat by more dominant groups. This can mean that they are scrutinised and regulated, which results in their dismissal. This invalidation of bisexual, pansex-ual, asexual, and plurisexual people perpetuates further erasure and invisibility (Chapter 3).

This book focused on specific examples of how bisexuality, pansexuality, asexuality, and plurisexualities are often invisible or invalidated within schools, workplaces, the mainstream mass media, and the wider culture (Chapters 3 and 5). This final chapter has outlined some of the ways in which bisexual, pansexual, asexual, and plurisexual people have made their sexualities visible to friends, family, and others, in their homes, and in physical and virtual spaces, and the opportunities that this offers in raising awareness and understanding of diverse sexualities. It has documented the considerable efforts of individuals, activists, academics, and organisations, to develop affirmative resources and create online and offline communities. These can be supportive of bisexual, pansexual, asexual, and plurisexual people and increase their visibility both through their existence and their specific content. While to be visible is not a straightforward route to becoming validated, nonetheless, to increase the visibility of bisexual, pansexual, asexual, and plurisexual identities is to increase the potential for these identities to become better recognised, represented, and understood by others and within the wider culture.

References

Andre, A., Brown, J., Delpercio, A., Kahn, E., Nicoll, A., & Sherouse, B. (2014, September 23). *Supporting and caring for our bisexual youth*. Washington, DC: Human Rights Campaign Foundation. Retrieved from https://hrc.org/youth-report/supporting-and-caring-for-our-bisexual-youth

Andrews, S. (2017, November 27). A brief history of the rainbow flag. Retrieved from www.thevintagenews.com/2017/11/27/a-brief-history-of-the-rainbow-flag-2/

Asexuality Archive (2012, February 20). The asexuality flag. Retrieved from www.asexualityarchive.com/the-asexuality-flag/

Bachmann, C. L., & Gooch, B. (2018). *LGBT in Britain: Homes and communities*. London: Stonewall.

Barefoot, K. N., Smalley, K. B., & Warren, J. C. (2017). Reproductive health and parenting in gender and sexual minority populations. In K. B. Smalley, J. C. Warren, & K. N. Barefoot (Eds.), *LGBT health: Meeting the needs of gender and sexual minorities* (pp. 103–126). New York: Springer. doi:10.1891/9780826133786.0007

Barker, M., Bowes-Catton, H., Iantaffi, A., Cassidy, A., & Brewer, L. (2008). British bisexuality: A snapshot of bisexual representations and identities in the United Kingdom. *Journal of Bisexuality, 8*(1–2), 141–162. doi:10.1080/15299710802143026

Barker, M., Richards, C., Jones, R., Bowes-Catton, H., & Plowman, T. (2012). *The bisexuality report: Bisexual inclusion in LGBT equality and diversity*. Milton Keynes: Open University, Centre for Citizenship, Identity, and Governance.

Bartelt, E., Bowling, J., Dodge, B., & Bostwick, W. (2017). Bisexual identity in the context of parenthood: An exploratory qualitative study of self-identified bisexual parents in the United States. *Journal of Bisexuality, 17*(4), 378–399. doi:10.1080/15299716.2017.1384947

Baxter-Williams, L. (2015, June 19). Hoisting our colours: A brief history of the bisexual pride flag. Retrieved from www.thisisbiscuit.co.uk/hoisting-our-colours-a-brief-history-of-the-bisexual-pride-flag/

Berbary, L. A., & Guzman, C. (2018). We exist: Combating erasure through creative analytic comix about bisexuality. *Qualitative Inquiry, 24*(7), 478–498. doi:10.1177/1077800417735628

Bernstein, M. (2002). Identities and politics: Toward a historical understanding of the lesbian and gay movement. *Social Science History*, 26(3), 531–581.

Bi Community News (BCN). (2019, October). BiCon's new working groups (may) want YOU! *Bi Community News* (BCN), 157.

Brown, M. F., & Lilton, D. L. (2019). Finding the "B" in LGBTQ+: Collections and practices that support the bisexual and pansexual communities. In B. Mehra (Ed.), *LGBTQ+ librarianship in the 21st century: Emerging directions of advocacy and community engagement in diverse information environments* (pp. 143–165). Bingley: Emerald. doi:10.1108/S0065-283020190000045013

Chasin, C. D. (2013). Reconsidering asexuality and its radical potential. *Feminist Studies*, 39(2), 405–426.

Clarke, V. (2016). Wearing a gay slogan T-shirt in the higher education classroom: A cautionary tale. *Feminism & Psychology*, 26(1), 3–10. doi:10.1177/0959353515613812

Clarke, V. (2019). "Some university lecturers wear gay pride T-shirts. Get over it!" Denials of homophobia and the reproduction of heteronormativity in responses to a gay-themed T-shirt. *Journal of Homosexuality*, 66(5), 690–714. doi:10.1080/00918369.2017.1423217

Compton, J. (2017, February 16). OutFront: #StillBisexual campaign founder fights for bi-visibility. Retrieved from www.nbcnews.com/feature/nbc-out/outfront-stillbisexual-campaign-founder-fights-bi-visibility-n721736

Cramer, E. P., & Gilson, S. F. (1999). Queers and crips: Parallel identity development processes for persons with nonvisible disabilities and lesbian, gay, and bisexual persons. *International Journal of Sexuality and Gender Studies*, 4(1), 23–37. doi:10.1023/A:1023250307175

Davies, D. (2000). Sharing our stories, empowering our lives: Don't dis me! *Sexuality and Disability*, 18(3), 179–186. doi:10.1023/A:1026465731431

Davila, J., Jabbour, J., Dyar, C., & Feinstein, B. A. (2019). Bi+ visibility: Characteristics of those who attempt to make their bisexual+ identity visible and the strategies they use. *Archives of Sexual Behavior*, 48(1), 199–211. doi:10.1007/s10508-018-1284-6

Dinwoodie, R., Greenhill, B., & Cookson, A. (2016). Them two things are what collide together": Understanding the sexual identity experiences of lesbian, gay, bisexual and trans people labelled with intellectual disability. *Journal of Applied Research in Intellectual Disabilities*, Advance online publication. doi:10.1111/jar.12252.

Feinstein, B. A., Dyar, C., Bhatia, V., Latack, J. A., & Davila, J. (2016). Conservative beliefs, attitudes toward bisexuality, and willingness to engage in romantic and sexual activities with a bisexual partner. *Archives of Sexual Behavior*, 45(6), 1535–1550. doi:10.1007/s10508-015-0642-x

Formby, E. (2012). *Solidarity but not similarity? LGBT communities in the twenty-first century*. Project Report. Sheffield: Sheffield Hallam University. Retrieved from http://shura.shu.ac.uk/6528/1/LGBT_communities_final_report_Nov2012.pdf

Foster, A. B., & Scherrer, K. S. (2014). Asexual-identified clients in clinical settings: Implications for culturally competent practice. *Psychology of Sexual Orientation and Gender Diversity*, 1(4), 422–430. doi:10.1037/sgd0000058

Garvey, J. C., Matsumura, J. L., Silvis, J. A., Kiemele, R., Eagan, H., & Chowdhury, P. (2018). Sexual borderlands: Exploring outness among bisexual, pansexual, and sexually fluid undergraduate students. *Journal of College Student Development*, 59(6), 666–680. doi:10.1353/csd.2018.0064

George, S. (2011). Blogging bisexuals and the coming-out process. *Journal of Bisexuality*, 11(2–3), 320–328. doi:10.1080/15299716.2011.572013

Ghabrial, M. A. (2017). "Trying to figure out where we belong": Narratives of racialized sexual minorities on community, identity, discrimination, and health. *Sexuality Research and Social Policy, 14*(1), 42–55. doi:10.1007/s13178-016-0229-x

Goldberg, A. E. (2010). *Lesbian and gay parents and their children: Research on the family life cycle.* Washington, DC: American Psychological Association. doi:10.1037/12055-000

Goldberg, A. E., Gartrell, N. K., & Gates, G. (2014, July). *Research report on LGB-parent families.* Los Angeles: Williams Institute. doi:10.1016/B978-0-12-800285-8.00003-0

Gonzalez, K. A., Ramirez, J. L., & Galupo, M. P. (2017). "I was and still am": Narratives of bisexual marking in the #StillBisexual campaign. *Sexuality & Culture, 21*(2), 493–515. doi:10.1007/s12119-016-9401-y

Gorman-Murray, A. (2006). Gay and lesbian couples at home: Identity work in domestic space. *Home Cultures, 3*(2), 145–167. doi:10.2752/174063106778053200

Gorman-Murray, A. (2007). Contesting domestic ideals: Queering the Australian home. *Australian Geographer, 38*(2), 195–213. doi:10.1080/00049180701392766

Gorman-Murray, A. (2008). Queering the family home: Narratives from gay, lesbian and bisexual youth coming out in supportive family homes in Australia. *Gender, Place and Culture, 15*(1), 31–44. doi:10.1080/09663690701817501

Gorman-Murray, A. (2012). Queer politics at home: Gay men's management of the public/private boundary. *New Zealand Geographer, 68*(2), 111–120. doi:10.1111/j.1745-7939.2012.01225.x

Gorman-Murray, A. (2015). Twentysomethings and twentagers: Subjectivities, spaces and young men at home. *Gender, Place & Culture, 22*(3), 422–439. doi:10.1080/0966369X.2013.879100

Grigorovich, A. (2015). Negotiating sexuality in home care settings: Older lesbians and bisexual women's experiences. *Culture, Health & Sexuality, 17*(8), 947–961. doi:10.1080/13691058.2015.1011237

Grov, C., Bimbi, D. S., Nanín, J. E., & Parsons, J. T. (2006). Race, ethnicity, gender, and generational factors associated with the coming-out process among gay, lesbian, and bisexual individuals. *Journal of Sex Research, 43*(2), 115–121. doi:10.1080/00224490609552306

Hartman, J. E. (2013). Creating a bisexual display: Making bisexuality visible. *Journal of Bisexuality, 13*(1), 39–62. doi:10.1080/15299716.2013.755727

Hayfield, N., Campbell, C., & Reed, E. (2018). Misrecognition and managing marginalisation: Bisexual people's experiences of bisexuality and relationships. *Psychology & Sexuality, 9*(3), 221–236. doi:10.1080/19419899.2018.1470106

Hayfield, N., Clarke, V., & Halliwell, E. (2014). Bisexual women's understandings of social marginalisation: "The heterosexuals don't understand us but nor do the lesbians". *Feminism & Psychology, 24*(3), 352–372. doi:10.1177/0959353514539651

Hitti, N. (2018, June 12). Daniel Quasar redesigns LGBT rainbow flag to be more inclusive. Retrieved from www.dezeen.com/2018/06/12/daniel-quasar-lgbt-rainbow-flag-inclusive/

Julia. (2016, October 28). A day in the life of a bi asexual. Retrieved from www.thisisbiscuit.co.uk/a-day-in-the-life-of-a-bi-asexual/

JustJasper. (2013, February 13). Confession time. Retrieved from https://justjasper.tumblr.com/post/42971325095/confession-time

Kattari, S. K. (2014). Sexual experiences of adults with physical disabilities: Negotiating with sexual partners. *Sexuality and Disability, 32*(4), 499–513. doi:10.1007/s11195-014-9379-z

Khayatt, D. (1997). Sex and the teacher: Should we come out in class? *Harvard Educational Review, 67*(1), 126–144. doi:10.17763/haer.67.1.27643568766g767m

Knous, H. M. (2006). The coming out experience for bisexuals: Identity formation and stigma management. *Journal of Bisexuality*, *5*(4), 37–59. doi:10.1300/J159v05n04_05

Lapointe, A. A. (2017). "It's not pans, it's people": Student and teacher perspectives on bisexuality and pansexuality. *Journal of Bisexuality*, *17*(1), 88–107. doi:10.1080/15299716.2016.1196157

Lovelock, M. (2019). "My coming out story": Lesbian, gay and bisexual youth identities on YouTube. *International Journal of Cultural Studies*, *22*(1), 70–85. doi:10.1177/1367877917720237

Lytle, A., Dyar, C., Levy, S. R., & London, B. (2017). Contact with bisexual individuals reduces binegativity among heterosexuals and lesbian women and gay men. *European Journal of Social Psychology*, *47*(5), 580–599. doi:10.1002/ejsp.2241

Maliepaard, E. (2018). Disclosing bisexuality or coming out? Two different realities for bisexual people in the Netherlands. *Journal of Bisexuality*, *18*(2), 145–167. doi:10.1080/15299716.2018.1452816

McCloskey, S. (2017). Brexit, Trump and development education. *Policy & Practice: A Development Education Review*, *24*, 159–168.

McCormack, M., Anderson, E., & Adams, A. (2014). Cohort effect on the coming out experiences of bisexual men. *Sociology*, *48*(6), 1207–1223. doi:10.1177/0038038513518851

McLean, K. (2007). Hiding in the closet? Bisexuals, coming out and the disclosure imperative. *Journal of Sociology*, *43*(2), 151–166. doi:10.1177/1440783307076893

Meeker, M. (2001). Behind the mask of respectability: Reconsidering the Mattachine Society and male homophile practice, 1950s and 1960s. *Journal of the History of Sexuality*, *10*(1), 78–116. doi:10.1353/sex.2001.0015

Meyer, R. (2006). Gay power circa 1970: Visual strategies for sexual revolution. *GLQ: A Journal of Lesbian and Gay Studies*, *12*(3), 441–464. doi:10.1215/10642684-2005-011

Monro, S. (2015). *Bisexuality: Identities, politics, and theories*. Basingstoke: Palgrave Macmillan.

Nerin. (2015, June 11). How common is the black ring? Retrieved from www.asexuality.org/en/topic/120367-how-common-is-the-black-ring/

Penney, J. (2013). Eminently visible: The role of T-shirts in gay and lesbian public advocacy and community building. *Popular Communication*, *11*(4), 289–302. doi:10.1080/15405702.2013.838251

Pew Research Center. (2013). *A survey of LGBT Americans: Attitudes, experiences and values in changing times*. Washington, DC: Author. Retrieved from www.pewsocialtrends.org/files/2013/06/SDT_LGBT-Americans_06-2013.pdf

Rasmussen, M. L. (2004). The problem of coming out. *Theory into Practice*, *43*(2), 144–150. doi:10.1207/s15430421tip4302_8

Rivers, I., & Gordon, K. (2010). "Coming out", context and reason: First disclosure of sexual orientation and its consequences. *Psychology & Sexuality*, *1*(1), 21–33. doi:10.1080/19419891003634398

Robbins, N. K., Low, K. G., & Query, A. N. (2016). A qualitative exploration of the "coming out" process for asexual individuals. *Archives of Sexual Behavior*, *45*(3), 751–760. doi:10.1007/s10508-015-0561-x

Ross, L. E., Dobinson, C., & Eady, A. (2010). Perceived determinants of mental health for bisexual people: A qualitative examination. *American Journal of Public Health*, *100*(3), 496–502. doi:10.2105/AJPH.2008.156307

Ross, L. E., Siegel, A., Dobinson, C., Epstein, R., & Steele, L. S. (2012). "I don't want to turn totally invisible": Mental health, stressors, and supports among bisexual women during the perinatal period. *Journal of GLBT Family Studies, 8*(2), 137–154. doi:10.1080/1550428X.2012.660791

Rothblum, E. D., Heimann, K., & Carpenter, K. (2019). The lives of asexual individuals outside of sexual and romantic relationships: Education, occupation, religion and community. *Psychology & Sexuality, 10*(1), 83–93. doi:10.1080/19419899.2018.1552186

Ruocco, C. (2014, June 16). Mashable publishes an up-to-date compilation of LGBT flags and symbols. Retrieved from www.glaad.org/blog/mashable-publishes-date-compil ation-lgbt-flags-and-symbols

Scherrer, K. S. (2017). Stigma and special issues for bisexual older adults. *Annual Review of Gerontology & Geriatrics, 37*, 43–57. doi:10.1891/0198-8794.37.43

Scherrer, K. S., Kazyak, E., & Schmitz, R. (2015). Getting "bi" in the family: Bisexual people's disclosure experiences. *Journal of Marriage and Family, 77*(3), 680–696. doi:10.1111/jomf.12190

Schroer, M. (2014). Visual culture and the fight for visibility. *Journal for the Theory of Social Behaviour, 44*(2), 206–228. doi:10.1111/jtsb.12038

Schultz, G. (2001). Daughters of Bilitis: Literary genealogy and lesbian authenticity. *GLQ: A Journal of Lesbian and Gay Studies, 7*(3), 377–389. doi:10.1215/10642684-7-3-377

See, H., & Hunt, R. (2011). Bisexuality and identity: The double-edged sword: Stonewall research into bisexual experience. *Journal of Bisexuality, 11*(2–3), 290–299. doi:10.1080/15299716.2011.571995

Stoffelen, J. M., Schaafsma, D., Kok, G., & Curfs, L. M. (2018). Women who love: An explorative study on experiences of lesbian and bisexual women with a mild intellectual disability in the Netherlands. *Sexuality and Disability, 36*(3), 249–264. doi:10.1007/s11195-018-9519-y

Townsend, M. (2016, October 8). Homophobic attacks in UK rose 147% in three months after Brexit vote. Retrieved from www.theguardian.com/society/2016/oct/08/homo phobic-attacks-double-after-brexit-vote

Wandrey, R. L., Mosack, K. E., & Moore, E. M. (2015). Coming out to family and friends as bisexually identified young adult women: A discussion of homophobia, biphobia, and heteronormativity. *Journal of Bisexuality, 15*(2), 204–229. doi:10.1080/15299716.2015.1018657

Westwood, S. (2016). "We see it as being heterosexualised, being put into a care home": Gender, sexuality and housing/care preferences among older LGB individuals in the UK. *Health & Social Care in the Community, 24*(6), e155–e163. doi:10.1111/hsc.12265

Whitney, C. (2006). Intersections in identity: Identity development among queer women with disabilities. *Sexuality and Disability, 24*(1), 39–52. doi:10.1007/s11195-005-9002-4

Willis, P., Maegusuku-Hewett, T., Raithby, M., & Miles, P. (2016). Swimming upstream: The provision of inclusive care to older lesbian, gay and bisexual (LGB) adults in resi dential and nursing environments in Wales. *Ageing & Society, 36*(2), 282–306. doi:10.1017/S0144686X14001147

Wolowic, J. M., Heston, L. V., Saewyc, E. M., Porta, C., & Eisenberg, M. E. (2017). Chasing the rainbow: Lesbian, gay, bisexual, transgender and queer youth and pride semiotics. *Culture, Health & Sexuality, 19*(5), 557–571. doi:10.1080/13691058.2016.1251613

INDEX

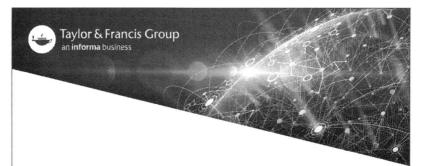